for IGCSE
Pearson
Edexcel

Religious Studies

Paper 2

Dr Adrian Samuel

My progress tracker

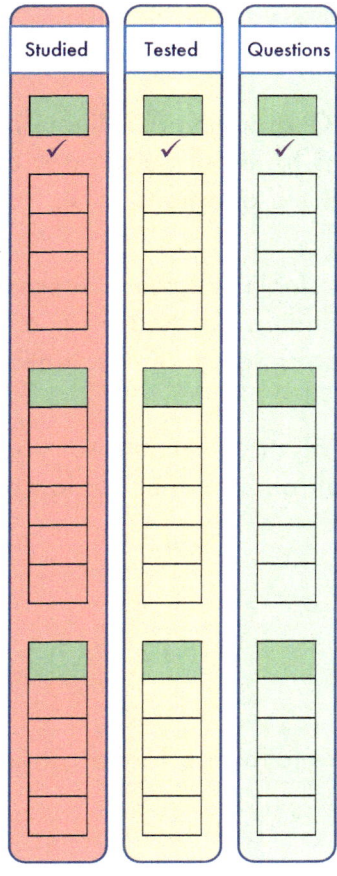

Paper 2: The Religious Community (Christianity)

Section 1: Origins and their Impact on the Community		
Unit	Title	Page
2.1.1a	Religious Texts	1
2.1.1b	Sources of Authority	12
2.1.2a	Founders and Leaders: Jesus	21
2.1.2b	Founders and Leaders: Martin Luther King	41

Section 2: Celebration and Pilgrimage		
2.2.1a	Festivals and Celebration: Christmas	46
2.2.1b	Festivals and Celebration: Easter	55
2.2.2a	Places of Pilgrimage: Bethlehem	62
2.2.2b	Places of Pilgrimage: Jerusalem	65
2.2.2c	Places of Pilgrimage: Vatican	71

Section 3: Worship and Practice		
2.3.1a	Places of Worship: Catholic	75
2.3.1b	Places of Worship: Baptists	84
2.3.2a	Forms of Worship: Catholic	89
2.3.2b	Forms of Worship: Baptists	98

IGCSE 2 Religious Studies

Exam technique.

REVISED ☐

- To learn best, you need to know how you will be tested on your learning.
- Paper 2 is worth 40% of your IGCSE qualification. (Paper 1, discussed in our companion textbook, counts as 60% of your qualification.)
- The Paper 2 examination lasts 1 ½ hours (assuming you do not have extra time) and is worth 60 marks. This means you have 1½ minute per mark.
- Paper 2 has 6 parts on the following religions: (A) Buddhism, (B) Christianity, (C) Hinduism, (D) Islam, (E) Judaism and (F) Sikhism. You answer all questions from **only one** part. So you have to turn to the religion of your choice and answer **all** the questions on it. You should ignore the questions on the other religions.
- This book focuses on RELIGION B: Christianity. This focus on a single religion is success-driven, allowing you to gain the detail and depth of understanding necessary for a 9 grade. (You can draw upon knowledge of other religions in answering certain evaluation questions, but this is not necessary.)
- For each religion, there are 3 sections and you need to answer **all** three sections for your chosen religion. (You cannot answer one section on one religion and another section on another religion.) The 3 sections are:

    o Section 1: Origins and their Impact on the Community
    o Section 2: Celebration and Pilgrimage
    o Section 3: Worship and Practice

- Each of the sections is assessed in terms of three questions in the following format. These are example questions from Section 1.

    (a) Outline **two** forms of leadership in the church. (4)
    (b) Explain how the baptism of Jesus is important for Christians. (6)
    (c) "The Bible is the only teaching a Christian needs."
    Discuss this statement considering the arguments for and against.
    In your answer you should include:
    • reference to teachings
    • other (divergent) points of view – either within the religion or from other religions
    • your opinion/point of view using reasoned arguments
    • a balanced conclusion. (10)

- Given that you have 1½ minute per mark, you should spend 6 minutes on the 4-marker (a) question. You should spend 9 minutes on the explanatory 6-marker (b) question. You should spend 15 minutes on the evaluative 10-marker (c) question. As a rule of thumb however, you should aim to finish the shorter questions more quickly so you have more time to answer the longer explanatory (6-mark) and evaluative (10-mark) questions.
- The way of answering each type of question is best demonstrated through example.

(a) Outline two forms of leadership in the church. (4)

- Identify a form of leadership (1st mark) and then briefly 'outline' or explain it to secure the 2nd mark. Repeat.
    - Roman Catholic leadership is guided by the pope, who shares in God's authority through 'apostolic succession'. [1] This is supported by Jesus' claim in Matthew 16 'You are Peter and upon this rock I shall build my church' (Matthew 16). The Pope is claimed to be the successor of Peter. [1]
    - Baptists believe in the *sola scriptura* doctrine following Martin Luther, which claims that scripture alone is necessary source for salvation. [1] Baptist leadership therefore involves Ministers who can help people understand the gospel (*evangelion* or 'good news') of how Christ atones for our sins and so brings salvation. [1]

(b) Explain how the baptism of Jesus is important for Christians. (6)

- As demonstrated below, your job for a 6-marker is to explain a position; you offer no judgment on the issue.
- You should aim to write 3 paragraphs following the PEE paragraph structure (point, explain, evidence).
- In each paragraph, you should firstly use the key concepts of the question in stating each of your points. (This is highlighted in red in the model answer.)
- Secondly, you need to explain each of your points. It is helpful to use the argument indicator phrase '*This is because ...*', since this indicates that you are giving a reason for your claim. (This is highlighted in purple in the first paragraph.)
- Thirdly, you need to show how your reasoning is grounded in an 'assured' knowledge of the religious tradition by referring to particular religious or scientific teachings. A useful argument indicator phrase is '*For example, ...*' since this allows you to select specific information relevant to your claim.
- Your answer is assessed in terms of the following Pearson Edexcel IGCSE mark scheme for a 6-mark explanatory question. 3 distinct points, each explained and supported by teachings will earn full marks since you will have demonstrated that your 'understanding' is 'assured' and 'comprehensive'.

IGCSE Mark Scheme

Mark	Descriptor
0	- No marks awarded.
1-3	- Some religious terms (AO1). - Beliefs & values are relevant and identified appropriately (AO2). - Some explanation of beliefs' and values' significance (AO2).
4-6	- Demonstrates understanding of religious terms (AO1). - Comprehensive account of beliefs and values, which are appropriately explained (AO2). - Confident & detailed account of beliefs and values as well as their significance (AO2).

IGCSE 2 Religious Studies

(d) "The Bible is the only teaching a Christian needs."
Discuss this statement including reasons for and against it.
Include in your answer:
- Discussion of teachings
- An opposed claim from either within that religion or from without
- Your judgment supported by reasons
- Conclusion that is persuasive. (10)

- Your job is to argue like a lawyer, defending your judgment against counter-arguments. As such, the method of answering this 10-mark question on Paper 2 is similar to the 12-mark evaluative question of Paper 1.

- The following model essay structure gives you a framework for writing your own essays.

- The letters DJCDJ stand for different paragraphs in your essay. You start your essay by defining what the question is about (D). You then make clear what you will be arguing for in your judgment (J). In your next paragraph, you consider criticisms of your position (C). You defend your judgment against those criticisms in the following paragraph. (D) You sum up in your concluding paragraph why your judgment is right, trying to persuade the reader of your position.

- You should avoid the temptation to merely offer two contrasting positions ('*On the one hand ...*') and then add your own opinion on at the end ('*In my opinion, ...* '). Similar to a lawyer, you are being judged on your skills in arguing for a position so your writing needs to be forceful, pointing out the weaknesses of the opposed position and persuading the reader of the correctness of your position. It is necessary to include counter-arguments to go beyond level 2.

- It is tempting to simply focus on what you are arguing for and ignore all the information you have learnt during your IGCSE. You need to avoid this temptation, and focus on *both* arguing for your position *and* on demonstrating how much knowledge you can integrate into your argument. To do this, think creatively about how many religious/scientific teachings you might use in the counter-arguments and defences you consider.

- You should structure the main paragraphs of your essay in terms of the PEEL (point, explain, evidence, link) method. The point uses the key concepts of the question to make clear what that paragraph will be arguing for. The explanation supports that point with a reason ('*This is because ...*'). The evidence sentence grounds your reasoning in the relevant facts ('*For example, ...*'). The link sentence ties your discussion back to the question, making clear to the reader how it addresses the question's key concepts ('*Therefore ...*'). This is best explained by way of the example below.

- The essay structure below gives you a framework for writing your own essays. The essay includes only a single counter-argument and a single defence. To aim for the highest marks, you should include more points. This will allow you to satisfy the mark scheme's demand for a 'comprehensive appraisal of evidence, leading to a fully justified conclusion'.

	Structure		'The Bible is the only teaching a Christian needs.' Discuss (10)
D	Definition		The Bible derives from the Greek word '*Biblia*' meaning books. These books were agreed by the Church councils to be 'canonical' for Christianity – i.e., they were necessary for understanding the Christian faith and so for salvation. These books are divided into two main sections. The first section the Old Testament, is understood to prophesy the coming of the Messiah (the promised leader who will reveal God's will on earth). The second section is the New Testament, revealing the goodness of God in His Son Jesus Christ, the 'incarnation' of the divine 'word' (John 1).
J	Judgment		It is mistaken to believe that the Bible is the only teaching a Christian needs since we can know God in a range of ways.
C	Criticism of judgment	P	Point (using key concepts of question) 'Against my position, Baptists would argue that the Bible is the only teaching a Christian needs.
		E	Explain ('This is because ...') This is because they believe that God communicates to us through 'special revelation': through prophets and His divine Son as recorded in scripture.
		E	Evidence (For example, ...) For example, they can appeal to the claim 'all scripture is God breathed'. (2 Timothy 3)
		L	Link (Therefore ... again using key concepts of question) Therefore Baptists would agree with Martin Luther's principle of '*sola scriptura*': only scripture is necessary for experiencing God's grace and so salvation.
D	Defence of judgment	P	Nevertheless, Roman Catholics seem to be correct in appealing to more than just special revelation.
		E	This is because, following St Thomas Aquinas' *Summa Theologica*, they also argue for natural revelation, in which we learn of God's purposes from studying nature.
		E	For example, by studying how humanity develops in a healthy way, we come to better understand how God intends for people to flourish.
		L	Therefore Aquinas' natural law theory is important in supplementing special revelation, allowing us to better understand God's purposes rather than reduce these to simple obedience to scripture.
J	Concluding judgment		In conclusion, it seems right that ... In conclusion, it seems right that the Bible is not the only teaching a Christian needs. Illuminated by the power of the Holy Spirit, which first descended upon the apostles as 'tongues of fire' (Acts 2), the Church has the ability to also discover God's purposes through a careful study of nature. Such 'natural revelation' allows the Church to better understand the 'mind of God' and so better interpret the Bible (special revelation).

IGCSE
Mark Scheme

Mark	Descriptor
0	No marks awarded.
1–3	• Understanding of religious views is very limited. • Attempt at connecting information in response to question, drawing upon some elements. • Judgements are supported by generic arguments to produce a conclusion that is not fully justified.
4–6	• Understanding of religious views is limited. • Analyses the information and attempts to make connections between some of the items of information relevant to the question. • Attempts to establish a judgment that is supported by an evaluation of some of the information, but this fails to fully justify its conclusion.
7–8	• Account of belief and religion is accurate. • Analyses relevant information and draws a clear and coherent conclusion while considering different views on the issue in question. The answer addresses some of the information relevant to the question. connections between many, but not all, of the elements in the question. • Argues for a coherent conclusion by drawing upon some of the information relevant to the question. There is some evaluation of the evidence and an attempt to integrate this into a developing argument.
9-10	• Accurate and comprehensive account of belief and religion. • Analyses information, drawing logically coherent conclusions, while responding to alternative positions. The answer addresses all of the information relevant to the question, integrating this into a developing argument. • Claims are fully justified and address all aspects of the question. The conclusion is drawn from a detailed evaluation of the evidence, integrating this into a developing argument for the conclusion.

Making the most of this book

- The section headings are taken directly from the Pearson Edexcel Exam Board syllabus.
- Sections are numbered so as to make clear which unit you are studying. So 2.1.1a means Paper 2, Section 1, Unit 1, first element.
- You should work through each unit, ticking it off on the Progress Tracker at the beginning of this book. You should firstly study it. You should then test yourself using the 'quiz' at the end of each unit. You should then use your knowledge to answer the questions at the end of each unit. On answering the questions, keep referring back to the essay structures discussed above.
- The Pearson Edexcel IGCSE specification includes two syllabuses. One is 'generic', identifying questions and topics that are required for answers on any religion. The other is a syllabus specific to each of the required religions. This book includes both the 'generic syllabus requirements' for any religion (in purple) and the specifically 'Christian syllabus requirements' (in deep blue). Seeing both alongside each other allows you to better predict what sort of questions you will be asked in the exam.

2.1 Origins & their impact on the community

Topic 2.1.1a Religious Texts

REVISED ☐

GENERIC SYLLABUS REQUIREMENTS
The authority and role of the religion's principal text(s) & its importance to the religious community. Its role in devotional worship & in education.

CHRISTIAN SYLLABUS REQUIREMENTS
The authority of the Bible for different Christians and their different interpretations of attitudes to the Bible. How the Bible is used by one Christian denomination in devotional worship & education.

Bible overview

REVISED ☐

The principal text of the Christianity is the Bible, which is judged to be 'canonical' for faith (i.e., authoritative for knowing the God of Christianity). The Bible includes the two main divisions: the Old Testament and the New Testament.

OLD TESTAMENT	NEW TESTAMENT
Scriptures shared with the Jewish faith about relationships (covenants) with God that are seen to be fulfilled in the promised 'Messiah' (literally 'anointed one' in Hebrew).	The uniquely Christian scriptures that concern the incarnation (God's becoming human) and a vision of the 'kingdom of God on earth as it is in heaven'.
TORAH — Hebrew for law: the first 5 books of the Bible (Genesis, Exodus, Leviticus, Numbers, Deuteronomy) present the key teachings of the Old Testament.	**GOSPELS** — 4 accounts of Jesus' life focused on his crucifixion. The synoptic Gospels of Matthew, Mark & Luke are very similar, but John's Gospel is distinctive. Gospel literally means 'good news'.
NEVI'IM — Hebrew for prophets, including the narrative prophets (such as Joshua, Samuel & Kings) and the latter prophets (such as Isaiah). They call us to live in a godly way.	**ACTS OF THE APOSTLES** — History of the early church after the ascension of Christ, written by Luke.
KETUVIM — Hebrew for writings, including the poetic meditations of Psalms, Proverbs & Job, which reflect upon our relationship to God.	**LETTERS & BOOK OF REVELATION** — Letters written by Church leaders (principally Paul) on how to follow Christ & so lead a godly life. The Book of Revelation prophesies the general resurrection & judgment at the end time.

IGCSE 2 Religious Studies

The Bible & its authority for Christians: the 'canon'

> **Key point**
>
> The Bible is a library of books, which the Christian community agreed best communicates their faith. This process of agreeing to 'canonical' or authorised texts involved rejecting some views (e.g., Marcion's) and agreeing with others (e.g., Athanasius'). It involved official statements of the canon (e.g., the Council of Rome) and later disagreement (e.g., Protestant rejections of the Deuterocanonical books).

- 'Canon' refers to the texts someone should have read for a subject. (e.g., Shakespeare is canonical for those studying English).
- The Christian canon refers to the agreed texts for knowing God in Christ. The Bible refers to the canonical books for this.
- In calling the Bible books 'canonical, the church is not claiming that other books should not be read. It is only claiming that those who claim to know God in Christ should have studied those books.
- The canon of Jewish scriptures was first described by the Jewish historian Josephus (37–100AD) in his work *Against Apion*.
- The Christian Church included the Jewish scriptures in their Old Testament as well as some later writings, which are often called the 'deuterocanonical' or 'intertestamental' writings. In contrast to the Hebrew Jewish scriptures, these 'deuterocanonical' writings were typically written later, but before Christ's birth. They are also typically in Greek.
- Marcion of Sinope (85–160AD) published the first known canon of the New Testament. It included only some of the Gospel of Luke and Paul's letters. Marcion was controversial however, since he rejected the Old Testament as canonical. Indeed, he characterises the creator God of the Old Testament as tribal and concerned with punishment whereas the God of Christianity is universal and concerned with love. The Church Councils rejected Marcion's arguments, seeing the Old Testament to also be canonical.
- Irenaeus of Lyon (c.130–c.202AD) was the first to refer to the 4 Gospels (the *Tetramorph*) as canonical.
- Origen (c. 184 – c. 253AD) is understood to have a Bible of the same 27 books as in the present New Testament canon.
- Bishop Athanasius of Alexandria in his Easter Letter of 367AD gives a list of books that would become the 27 books of the New Testament canon and uses the word 'canonised' to refer to them.
- The Council of Rome (AD 382) went on to define this list of books canonical, making up the Christian Bible.
- With the Reformation, Martin Luther (1483–1546) rejected treating the deuteron-canonical books of the Old Testament as canonical since these books did not have Hebrew originals (due to being written in Greek as discussed above). Luther referred to them as *apocrypha*: "books which are not considered equal to the Holy Scriptures, but are useful and good to read." Most Protestants followed Martin Luther in not treating the 'intertestamental writings' as canonical.

- The Catholic Church and Eastern Orthodox Church rejected Luther's claims, affirming both the Hebrew and Greek Old Testament books as 'canonical'.
- In Western Christendom (Roman Catholic countries), the Bible used to be read in Latin in the authorised 'Vulgate' translation. With the rise of Protestantism however, the Bible was read in the 'vernacular' (local language). Roman Catholicism allowed for Bible readings in the vernacular after the 2nd Vatican Council (1962-5). Eastern Orthodox countries have always allowed for Bible readings in the vernacular

The Bible and its authority for Christians: its contents   REVISED ☐

> **Key point**
> Different books of the Bible have different authority. The Old Testament books prophesy that we can share in the life of God. The New Testament presents us with the character of the life of God as revealed in Christ. Christians therefore see the New Testament to have greater authority than the Old Testament. Further, different books within the Old and New Testaments have different authority. In the Old Testament, the 1st 5 books (the *Torah*) have the greatest authority since these include the key teachings ('law'). In the New Testament, the 4 Gospels have the greatest authority since these directly present the life of God revealed in Christ.

- The Bible includes the Old and the New Testaments.

THE OLD TESTAMENT
- The Old Testament is made up of the 24 books of the Jewish Hebrew scriptures as well as the Deuterocanonical books (Jewish scriptures typically written in Greek, but which are not accepted as canonical by the Jewish religion).
- In the 16th century AD, the Protestant Churches rejected the 'deuterocanonical' scriptures as 'canonical', labelling them instead 'intertestamental' writings or 'apocrypha' (literally hidden writings). This is because they had now Hebrew original.
- The Roman Catholic and Eastern Orthodox Churches continue to see the deuterocanonical books as canonical.
- Within the Old Testament, the 'Torah' (first 5 books) has the greatest authority.
  1. Genesis, in particular, includes key teachings such as the creation of the world (Genesis 1 & 2), the flood and Noah's ark (Genesis 9), the beginning of the people of God with Abraham (Genesis 17) and Joseph's saving them (Genesis 37-45).
  2. Exodus describes the Jews being freed from slavery in Egypt under the direction of Moses and their being given the 10 commandments on Mount Sinai. (Exodus 20)
  3. Leviticus describes practices of moral and ritual purification.
  4. Numbers describes the suffering of the people of God (the Jews) and their failure to be grateful to God.
  5. Deuteronomy is a farewell address by Moses to the Israelites (Jews) before they enter the promised land of Canaan.

- The **Nevi'im** or Prophets (literally spokesmen) is of second greatest importance in the Old Testament: this is divided into the Former Prophets and the Latter Prophets. The Former Prophets (e.g., Joshua, Judges & Samuel) continue the narrative after the death of Moses. The Latter Prophets challenge the Jewish people to live a more godly life (e.g., Isaiah, Jeremiah, Amos and Hosea).
- The **Ketuvim** are the 'writings' or 'wisdom literature' of the Old Testament and these are of third importance. These are not historical but stories to deepen our understanding of God. The Psalms are songs of coming to know God, attributed to King Solomon. The Book of Job is a meditation on evil and how it is impossible for us to explain why it exists. The Book Proverbs are sayings about how to live.

THE NEW TESTAMENT

- **The Gospels** are of central authority in the Bible as they present the life of God that Christians are called to share in.
    1. The **Synoptic Gospels** are three accounts of Jesus' life by Matthew, Mark and Luke. Each of these essentially agree in presenting Jesus' teachings in terms of parables about the 'kingdom of God', although each has a different focus.
        - Matthew's Gospel: focuses on how Jesus is the fulfilment of Jewish prophecy.
        - Mark's Gospel: focuses on the drama of Jesus' ministry.
        - Luke's Gospel: focuses on Jesus' ministry to those
    2. The **4th Gospel** (**John's Gospel**): presents Jesus' teachings in terms of the 'I am' sayings – e.g., 'I am the way, the truth and the life' (John 14), 'I am the vine; you are the branches' (John 15), 'I am the good shepherd ... I lay down my life for the sheep' (John 10).
- The **Acts of the Apostles** is also written by Luke and describes the early history of the Christian church. It presents the apostles coming to share in the power that Jesus did (the power of the Holy Spirit) on the day of Pentecost and their leading the Christian community to live lives faithful to God. Although not as significant as the Gospels, this remains central for an understanding of the Christian faith.
- The **Letters** are actual letters written by Church leaders guiding Christian communities on how to lead lives faithful to God. Of particular importance are the letters of Paul:
    1. Letters to the Romans and the Galatians make 'justification by faith' rather than 'justification by works'. Justification here means not proving one's point, but one's being made just (i.e., sharing in God's justice). Paul argues that to share in God's justice, Christians do not perform works obedient to the 613 rules of the Old Testament; they rather need to share in God's life revealed in Christ by living lives of faith. The letters have greater authority than the Old Testament, but less authority than the Gospels.
- The Book of **Revelation** is a vision of the end time (in Greek '*eschaton*') in which there is the 'second coming' of Jesus (in Greek '*parousia*') and the 'general resurrection' in which all receive 'spiritual bodies' and are judged by God, only sharing in the new creation if their lives have pleased God. If their lives have displeased God, they suffer hell. The authority of the Book of Revelation is interpreted differently; the futurists see it to foresee future events. Historicists see the Book to present a Christian vision of history as a whole. The Book of Revelation was one of the last books to be accepted into the canon.

The Bible as God's word

> **Key point**
>
> Christianity has a threefold understanding of the 'word' of God. There is the eternal 'word', which is the eternal 'Son of God' which is God (according to the Trinity). There is the historical 'word' revealed through the prophets and fulfilled in the incarnation – God's word or Son becomes flesh in Jesus. And there is the recorded 'word' of the Bible, which allows us to understand both the eternal and historical 'word' of God and so share in the life of God.

- The Bible has traditionally been interpreted as the 'word of God'.
- The 'word' in the 'word of God' translates the Greek *logos* meaning speech or understanding.
- This 'word' is claimed to be eternal, existing before creation: 'In the beginning was the Word, and the Word was with God, and the Word was God.' (John 1)
- This 'word' is also identified with the eternal 'Son of God' who is God. [See my IGCSE Religious Studies Book 1 on the Trinity: God is Father, Son and Holy Spirit.]
- This eternal 'word' has been historically revealed in the 'covenants' or agreements between God and humanity established through the prophets. These covenants are 'fulfilled' by the 'new covenant' (Mark 14), which reveals not just the message of God, but the character of God in Christ: 'And the Word was made flesh, and dwelt among us full of grace and truth.' (John 1)
- The Bible is the recorded word of God that allows us to understand both the eternal 'word' and the historical 'word' of God: 'All Scripture is God-breathed and is useful for teaching, rebuking, correcting and training in righteousness.' (2 Timothy 3) [This is one of the letters in the New Testament to Timothy, which was traditionally thought to have been written by Paul]
- Christians do not therefore claim that the Bible was dictated by God (as Muslims claim of their Qur'an). At the heart of the Christian faith is incarnation not dictation. Nevertheless, the Bible is the inspired 'word' or understanding of God allowing us to share in the life of God revealed in Christ.
- Different Christians understand the Bible's inspiration differently. Roman Catholic and evangelical Christians (e.g., Baptists) typically see the Bible to be 'infallible' (completely trustworthy) and 'inerrant' (without error). For example, the Catholic Second Vatican Council (1962–5) writes: "Since everything asserted by the inspired authors or sacred writers must be held to be asserted by the Holy Spirit, it follows that the books of Scripture must be acknowledged as teaching solidly, faithfully and without error that truth which God wanted put into sacred writings for the sake of salvation."
- More liberal Christians (e.g., many Church of England Christians and Quakers) see the Bible to be 'infallible' (completely trustworthy for salvation) but not inerrant (without error). These Christians therefore allow that the Bible is not mistaken on its spiritual claims (i.e., that we should live lives of 'faith, hope and love' (1 Corinthians 13)). Nevertheless, it can be mistaken on certain factual claims (e.g., its belief in miracles).

Traditional interpretations of the Bible   REVISED ☐

- Traditionally the Bible has been interpreted to be both 'infallible' (a trustworthy guide to salvation) and 'inerrant' (without error).
- James L. Kugel summarises traditional and historical Biblical interpretation in his book *'How to Read the Bible: a guide to scripture then and now.'*
- For traditional Biblical interpretation, the Bible was seen to be 'inerrant' at a literal (factual level) and 'infallible' (trustworthy) in its moral and spiritual guidance. Developing this position, Thomas Aquinas (1225–74) appeal to 4 levels of Biblical interpretation, which we can illustrate regarding the Parable of the Good Samaritan (see below):
  1. Literal (what is said – its information) – e.g., the parable of the Good Samaritan is about a man who is assaulted and finally helped.
  2. Allegorical (what it means – the understanding it offers) – e.g., the parable answers the question 'Who is my neighbour?" as follows: "The one who is merciful."
  3. Moral (what we should do) – e.g., the parable tells us that we should be merciful: "Go and do likewise."
  4. Spiritual (what we should hope for) – e.g., the parable holds up a vision of a better world in which we are not selfish, but caring.
- In the case of the Good Samaritan, it is a parable, so it is not understood to be literally true given its context (i.e., its being deliberately presented as a made-up story). Much of the Bible however (e.g., the creation stories of Genesis 1 & 2) were seen to be literally true while also having deeper allegorical, moral and spiritual messages.

The Parable of the Good Samaritan

On one occasion an expert in the law stood up to test Jesus. "Teacher," he asked, "what must I do to inherit eternal life?"

"What is written in the Law?" he replied. "How do you read it?"

He answered, "'Love the Lord your God with all your heart and with all your soul and with all your strength and with all your mind'; and, 'Love your neighbour as yourself.'"

"You have answered correctly," Jesus replied. "Do this and you will live."

But he wanted to justify himself, so he asked Jesus, "And who is my neighbour?"

In reply Jesus said: "A man was going down from Jerusalem to Jericho, when he was attacked by robbers. They stripped him of his clothes, beat him and went away, leaving him half dead. A priest happened to be going down the same road, and when he saw the man, he passed by on the other side. So too, a Levite, when he came to the place and saw him, passed by on the other side. But a Samaritan, as he traveled, came where the man was; and when he saw him, he took pity on him. He went to him and bandaged his wounds, pouring on oil and wine. Then he put the man on his own donkey, brought him to an inn and took care of him. The next day he took out two denarii and gave them to the innkeeper. 'Look after him,' he said, 'and when I return, I will reimburse you for any extra expense you may have.'

"Which of these three do you think was a neighbour to the man who fell into the hands of robbers?"

The expert in the law replied, "The one who had mercy on him."

Jesus told him, "Go and do likewise."

(Luke 10:25–37)

Modern interpretations of the Bible

> **Key point**
>
> If the ancient interpretations of the Bible treated the Bible as a source of authority, examining its literal, allegorical, moral and spiritual messages, modern interpretations of the Bible treat it as a historical document. Fundamentalists have rejected such an understanding, insisting that Bible should be seen as a source of authority and many of its 'truths' are fundamental for real faith. Atheists have agreed that the Bible is a historical document and has no sacred authority. Liberal Christians have attempted to argue that the Bible is a historical document, but one that reveals eternal truths.

- With the development of universities, devotional readings of the Bible in monasteries and convents according to the traditional method of interpretation came to be challenged by more academic readings of the Bible in the 17th to 20thc AD. This gave rise to what is called 'Historical Criticism' or 'Higher Criticism'. Instead of interpreting the different levels of truth revealed by scripture, Historical Criticism was more critical, investigating the historical sources of the Bible's claims. Historical criticism involved two main methods:

- **Form Criticism**: this approach to historical criticism examines the style of writing. This has led scholars to adopt the 'documentary hypothesis', which challenges the traditional claim that Moses was the author of the first 5 books of the Old Testament (the 'Torah' or Law of Judaism). Stylistic differences now lead scholars to conclude that these books were written by 4 separate authors referred to as JEPD. This explains why there are 2 creation stories in Genesis – the 'E' author (who refers to God as 'Elohim') wrote Genesis 1 and the 'J' author (who refers to God as Jehovah) wrote Genesis 2 and these different accounts were edited together. Form Criticism has therefore challenged the traditional claim that the 'Holy Spirit' is the 'infallible' and 'inerrant' author of the Bible – the Bible rather has different claims written in different styles allowing us to analyse the multiple authors of even single books (e.g., Genesis).

- **Source Criticism**: this approach to historical criticism examines the historical sources of the Bible. Examining the Gospels of the New Testament, it claims that certain Gospels used information from other Gospels (i.e., certain sections are copied since they are identical). They concluded that the Gospels of Luke and Matthew partially copied from the Gospel of Mark and another lost document ('Q') since they seem to have identical passages that are best explained by this 'two-source hypothesis'. This challenges any claim that the Bible was written by Holy Spirit since it seems to have been written on the basis of historical sources, some of which are available to use (Mark's Gospel) and some of which have been lost ('Q').

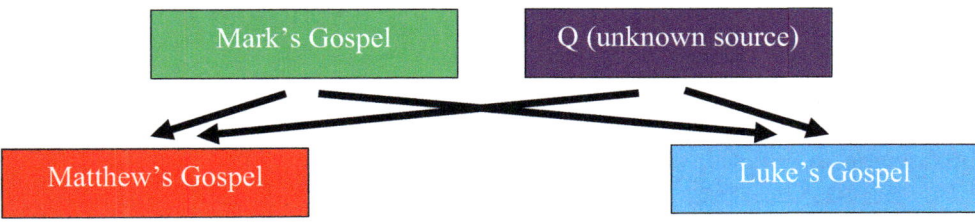

IGCSE 2 Religious Studies

- The results of historical criticism are varied:

1. Many people concluded that faith was not real, appealing to naturalism. They argued that there were historical explanations for everything – including belief in God. Ludwig Feuerbach (1804–1872) in his book *The Essence of Christianity* powerfully argued for the 'anthropological essence of religion', which treats God as 'a being of the understanding' – i.e., an ideal we have made up. In other words, God has not made us in his image, but we have made God in our own idealised image.
2. The Christian 'fundamentalist' movement reacted against source and historical criticism, defending scripture's 'inerrancy' on certain 'fundamental' literal claims – e.g., the 'virgin birth' of Jesus and his coming back from the dead in his 'resurrection'. In *The Fundamentals: a testimony to truth* (1910–15), Evangelical Protestants published a series of 12 pamphlets attacking modernist theories of biblical criticism and defending the authority of the Bible. Such groups were often attacked as uneducated and narrow-minded by their opponents, although this was not completely fair.
3. Some Liberal Christians, like Rudolf Bultmann (1884–1976), accepted 'historical criticism', and they agreed with the atheists that supernatural events in the Bible (e.g., miracles) are not literally true. They explain miracles as beliefs common to their age (e.g., magic was widely accepted as real by everybody in ancient civilisations – not just Christians). Nevertheless, Bultmann argued that there are eternal truths in the Bible that cannot be see as mere historical events. These are the real message ('kerygma') of the Christian faith – e.g., we should live according to the 'theological virtues' of 'faith, hope and love' (1 Corinthians 13).

To avoid confusion, Bultmann therefore argued that we need to 'demythologize' the Bible. In other words, we need to reject reading the Bible literally in terms of supernatural events (miracles). We should rather read the Bible in terms of its eternal message ('kerygma') – its witnessing to life's meaning (allegorical interpretation), its responsibility (moral interpretation) and its hope (spiritual interpretation).

For example, Bultmann understood the resurrection not as a 'literal' or historical event (i.e., Jesus was not literally resuscitated from the dead). Bultmann saw the resurrection as an 'eschatological' event, – an 'end time' or overarching purpose of life, understood as its overcoming sin and death in a 'new creation' (Revelation 21).

> **Your judgment**
> Try to decide which position you believe.
> 1. Do you agree with the fundamentalists that the Bible should be treated as a revelation of divine authority and not as a historical document?
> 2. Do you agree with the atheists that the Bible is one historical document amongst others and has no sacred authority?
> 3. Do you agree with Rudolf Bultmann that the Bible reveals a sacred message ('kerygma') even if that message needs to be extracted from the scientifically incorrect 'myths' of the age in which it was written?

One denomination's use of the Bible.

> **Key point**
>
> Roman Catholicism uses the Bible in worshipping God, in praying, in structuring the Church year, in legitimating its own authority to speak in the name of God and in giving guidance on how people should live

- **Worship** – The Bible is used as a basis for Catholic ritual – e.g., Catholic 'masses' are divided into the liturgy of the 'word' (Bible readings and sermons inspired by those readings) and the liturgy of the 'sacrament' (the ritual of sharing in the body and blood of Christ, which re-enacts the story of Jesus' Last Supper in the Bible.)

- **Pastoral services** – services like weddings and funerals include Bible readings. The nature of each of the services is also shaped by the Bible's teachings on marriage and on death. For example, weddings see marriage to involve an eternal bond of love, following Jesus' teachings in the Bible. Funerals see death to involve our sharing in the afterlife, again following Jesus' teachings in the Bible.

- **Lectionary** – the Christian calendar is structured around Biblical (e.g., the year begins with Advent as the lead-up to Christmas, which itself celebrates the birth of Christ as recorded in scripture. The lectionary are Bible readings for each day in this calendar, allowing all the books of the Bible to be read in services.

- **Prayer** – the Bible is used to structure prayer. For example, the 'breviary' (a book of prayers for priests, monks and nuns) includes prayers for each day, including Bible passages, psalms and the Lord's prayer (Matthew 6 & Luke 11). Services also regularly include 'canticles' such as the 'Song of Simeon' [called the '*Nunc Dimittis*'] (Luke 2) and 'Mary's song' [called the '*Magnificat*'] (Luke 1), which both celebrates the incarnation. The Catholic Rosary is a set of beads to structure private mediation on events in the Bible (the 'Joyful Mystery' of the incarnation, the 'Sorrowful Mystery' of the crucifixion and the 'Glorious Mystery' of the resurrection).

- **Hymns** – the Catholic Church includes hymn singing in worship and in prayer, and these songs are typically inspired by passages in the Bible (e.g., 'The Lord's My Shepherd') or by key concepts in the Bible (e.g., 'Amazing Grace')

- **Legitimating the Catholic tradition** – just as God gives his authority to Jesus, Jesus passes on some of his authority to his apostle Peter: 'You are Peter, and upon this rock I will build my church.' (Matthew 16) Further, Peter as the first Bishop of Rome passes his authority to future Bishops of Rome (Popes) who grant authority to priests to speak in God's name. 'I will give you the keys of the kingdom of heaven; whatever you bind on earth will be bound in heaven, and whatever you loose on earth will be loosed in heaven.' (Matthew 16) This allows priests to forgive sins in God's name in the sacrament of Confession or Reconciliation.

- **Encyclicals** – teaching letters from the Pope to priests on what the Catholic faith teaches. The Pope typically supports his claims by appealing to the teachings of the Bible. (e.g., Pope Francis' encyclical *Lumen Fidei* or Light of Faith "speaks of the great gift brought by Jesus." (2013

IGCSE 2 Religious Studies

Recall the definitions ... quiz yourself both ways!

TESTED ☐

Key word	Definition
Bible	Library of books that are judged to be 'canonical'
Canonical	Books judged by the Church to be sacred & so are central for faith
Old Testament	The Bible's Hebrew Jewish Scriptures (Protestants) and the Greek Deutero-canonical books (Catholicism and Eastern Orthodoxy)
Torah	Hebrew for Law or teaching: the first 5 books of the Bible that are seen to be the most authoritative part of the Old Testament
Nevi'im	Hebrew for Prophets, referring to a range of writings on the history of the 'people of God' (Jews) in the Old Testament
Ketuvim	Hebrew for 'writings' and often concerns meditations (e.g., poetry or stories) on the nature of God
Hebrew	The original Jewish language of much of the Old Testament
Messiah	The Hebrew word for 'anointed one' (a leader blessed using sacred oils) who is prophesied in the Old Testament.
Christ	Greek translation of Messiah
New Testament	The Bible's Greek scriptures that describe the life of Jesus and what it means to share in God's life revealed in Christ. This is more authoritative for Christianity than the Old Testament.
Gospels	Literally 'good news', describing the incarnation of the life of God in Jesus Christ and the overcoming of sin and death (resurrection). This is the most authoritative section of the Bible.
Synoptic Gospels	The Gospels of Matthew, Mark and Luke, which present Jesus' teachings in terms of parables (stories) about the 'kingdom of God'
4th Gospel	The Gospel of John, which presents Jesus' teachings in terms of 'I am' sayings focused on the incarnation
Incarnation	The eternal 'word' or 'Son' of God becomes 'flesh' (human) in Jesus
Acts	The life of the early Church and its sharing in the authority of the Holy Spirit. This is written by Luke, the author of one of the Gospels.
Letters (epistles)	Authoritative letters by Church leaders on what it means to follow Christ in the way one lives.
Justification by faith	Paul, author of many of the Bible's letters, argues that sharing in the life of God ('justification by faith') replaces the need to obey the 613 rules of Judaism ('justification by works')
Book of Revelation	Last book of the New Testament, giving a vision of the end time ('eschaton') with the second coming ('parousia') of Jesus to judge everyone and bring about the 'general resurrection'
Resurrection	The overcoming of sin and death with souls being restored to 'spiritual bodies' (1 Corinthians 15)
Logos (word)	Speech or understanding, which is eternal (as God the Son), historical (as prophetic and incarnation) and recorded (as Bible).
Infallible	Completely trustworthy
Inerrant	Without error
James Kugel	Author of *How to Read the Bible: a guide to scripture then and now*
Ancient interpretation	Reading the Bible as a source of authority (whose author is the Holy Spirit) and which needs to be interpreted on multiple levels

211a Religious Texts

IGCSE 2 Religious Studies

Key word	Definition
Literal	What it says – factual
Allegorical	What it means – understanding
Moral	What we should do – guidance on how to live
Spiritual	What we should hope for – the purpose of life.
Parable of the Good Samaritan	A parable about a man who is attacked and helped by the foreigner (Samaritan) helping us to understand 'Who is my neighbour?
Modern interpretation	'Historical' or 'higher' criticism, treating the Bible not as a source of authority but as a historical document
Form criticism	Analyses the different writing styles of the Bible to discover who wrote what where and when.
Torah's authorship	Traditionally claimed to be authored by Moses through the power of the Holy Spirit, but Form Criticism claims that it has multiple authors labelled J (Yahwistic author), E (Elohistic author), P (priestly author) and D (Deuteronomistic author)
Source criticism	Analyses the historical sources of the Bible, concluding that certain books were used to write other books
Two-source hypothesis	Noticing identical sections in scripture, Source Criticism concluded that Matthew and Luke copied sections from Mark and a lost document 'Q'.
Fundamentalist	Rejects historical criticism, claiming that certain factual claims (e.g., literal resurrection of Jesus from the dead) needed to be accepted on faith and not seen as historically made up.
Naturalism	Rejects supernatural explanations of the Bible (e.g., the Holy Spirit as the source of scripture) in favour of historical explanations.
Fundamentalism	Rejects naturalistic explanations of the Bible, claiming that 'fundamental' Biblical claims such as the literal resurrection of Christ were 'inerrant'.
Rudolf Bultmann	We could 'demythologise' the mistaken beliefs of the Biblical authors (e.g., a belief in magic or miracles) so as to discover the Bible's eternal message ('kerygma').
Catholicism's use of Bible	Used for worship (mass), prayer (breviary & rosary), writing hymns, legitimating Catholic claims to authority, writing Encyclicals.

TESTED

Test yourself

Done

(a) Outline **two** parts of the Bible. (4)
(b) Explain different ways in which the Bible is interpreted. (6)
(c) "The Bible is the only teaching a Christian needs."
Discuss this statement considering the arguments for and against.
   In your answer you should include:
- reference to teachings
- other (divergent) points of view – either within the religion or from other religions
- your opinion/point of view using reasoned arguments
- a balanced conclusion. (10)

IGCSE 2 Religious Studies

2.1.1b Sources of Authority

GENERIC SYLLABUS REQUIREMENTS
The different religious sources of authority.

CHRISTIAN SYLLABUS REQUIREMENTS
Different Christian attitudes to sources of authority, including personal conscience, the ordained ministry, the laity and leadership amongst local communities. One Christian denomination's understanding of religious authority.

Authority in Catholicism.

> **Key point**
>
> **Roman Catholicism** sees there to be one truth revealed in 4 distinct ways – through scripture, tradition, reason and experience. Although each strand of revelation is distinct, each is meant to reinforce the others, similar to the strands of a rope.

- Catholicism appeals to four distinct strands of authority: scripture, tradition, reason and experience. Its position draws upon the work of St Thomas Aquinas' (1225–74). Pope Leo XIII claimed in his encyclical *Aeterni Patris* of 1879 that Thomas Aquinas' theology was definitive for Catholic doctrine (teaching).
- **SCRIPTURE**: Catholicism gives great importance to the Bible (scripture) seeing it to be an 'infallible' (completely trustworthy) and 'inerrant' (without error) source of authority.
- Catholicism typically interprets the Bible as a divine revelation and not as a series of historical events (characteristic of Historical Criticism). Its interpretation of the Bible is therefore quite traditional, typically treating the literal message (e.g., Jesus rose from the dead) as factually accurate, although to properly understand what is being revealed in this, we need to interpret it allegorically morally and spiritually. As we saw above, Catholicism declared the Bible to be 'inerrant' in its Second Vatican Council of 1962-5, writing: 'Scripture must be acknowledged as teaching solidly, faithfully and without error that truth which God wanted put into sacred writings for the sake of salvation.'
- Unlike the Protestants however, who tended to reject all other forms of authority except scripture in their *sola scriptura* belief of Martin Luther (16c) [see below], Catholics allow for other forms of revelation.
- **TRADITION**: the Church is believed to act under divine inspiration, similar to how individual prophets act under divine inspiration.
- Under divine inspiration, the Church judged which books are 'canonical' and so should be included in the Bible (e.g., Council of Rome in 382AD).
- The Bible itself describes how the apostles received the divine inspiration of the Holy Spirit on the day of Pentecost in Acts 2. Experiencing 'tongues of fire', they were empowered with the Holy Spirit.
- The apostles also shared in God's healing power, with Peter healing the lame man in the Temple, as recorded in Acts 3.

- The Catholic Church claims to share in this power of God revealed through Christ. As noted above, just as God gives his authority to Jesus, Jesus passes on some of his authority to his apostle Peter: 'You are Peter, and upon this rock I will build my church.' (Matthew 16) Through 'apostolic succession', Popes are spiritual successors of Peter, guided by the Holy Spirit to 'ordain' church leaders (priests) to lead the 'laity' (congregations) in how to share in the life of God revealed in Christ.

- The Councils of the Church have agreed basic ideas in terms of which to interpret scripture and created 'creeds' [statements of belief] summarising these. For example, the Nicene Creed (325AD) defines the central idea of the 'Trinity' for understanding scripture's account of God as Father, Son and Holy Spirit.

- The power of the Holy Spirit enables priests to perform sacramental duties. Sacraments are "the visible form of an invisible grace" (Augustine). For example, priests can forgive people of their sins in the Sacrament of Confession, following Matthew 16: 'I will give you the keys of the kingdom of heaven; whatever you bind on earth will be bound in heaven, and whatever you loose on earth will be loosed in heaven.' (Matthew 16) This allows priests to forgive sins in God's name in the sacrament of Confession or Reconciliation.

- This special authority of the Pope allows him to even declare certain beliefs as necessary for Catholics to believe. For example, Pope Pius IX declared in his Encyclical *Ineffabilis Deus* of 1854 that the teaching of the 'immaculate conception' was a required church teaching ('dogma'). This is the belief that Mary the mother of Jesus was born without 'original sin', even though there is no reference to this in the Bible.

> **Mistake to avoid**
> Do not confuse the 'immaculate conception' of Mary with the 'Virgin Birth' of Jesus.

- Priests also share in the power of enacting the 'real presence' of God in the Eucharist or Mass. When they say the 'words of consecration' ['Take eat this is my body which is given for you' and 'This is my blood which is shed for you and for many for the forgiveness of sins'], there is 'transubstantiation'. In this ritual, the bread literally becomes the body of Christ and the wine becomes the blood of Christ, allowing Catholics to directly experience the 'real presence' of God through the Catholic tradition and its liturgy.

- REASON – Aquinas, in his *Summa Theologica*, argued for 'Natural Law Theory'. This claims that reasoning (independent of the Bible) can give a functional analysis of things – e.g., through reasoning we note that the function of the legs is to walk and run. Further, Aquinas argues that we can discover what helps something function better ('flourish') and what damages it. For example, the body functions better with exercise and is damaged by eating too much. Finally, Aquinas argues, God intends for things to flourish and not be damaged. By going against something's proper function, we are therefore going against God's purposes for it. Damaging oneself (suicide) has therefore traditionally been a sin – damaging the gift of life that God has given you instead of allowing it to flourish.

- Based upon Aquinas' Natural Law Theory, contraception and masturbation have traditionally been seen as sinful since these reproductive organs have a reproductive function. To separate the pleasure of sex from its role in the creation of new life results in our failing to use sex for the right purpose. The Bible itself, by contrast, does not directly discuss either of these topics. Aquinas therefore clearly distinguishes 'special revelation' (the revelation of scripture) from 'natural revelation' (the revelation of reason). Each can reveal to us different things. Nevertheless, Aquinas did not believe that the truths of reason could ever contradict the truths of scripture – for God is 'the sovereign and first truth (*Summa Theologica* 1: 16: 5).

- **EXPERIENCE** – Aquinas argued that conscience is the direct experience of God speaking in us. This is because within each one of us there is the power of '*synderesis*' – 'the law of our mind' (*Summa Theologica* 1,2: 94: 1). This directs us towards goodness and away from evil. On the basis of this experience of goodness, we develop 'primary precepts' or principles on how to live (e.g., 'protect and preserve human life') and 'secondary precepts' on how to enact these principles (e.g., 'Do not kill').

- Again, the experience of conscience cannot contradict the demands of natural law or scripture since there is only one truth for Aquinas which is God. For example, the secondary precept 'Do not kill' is reinforced by the 6th commandment 'Do not kill' (Exodus 20) which is reinforced by natural law theory's concern that people should flourish and not die and which is reinforced by the tradition's witness throughout history to the 'sanctity of life' (all human life is sacred).

Eastern Orthodox Church.

> **Key point**
>
> The Eastern Orthodox Church is a conservative denomination, believing in the 'infallible' and 'inerrant' authority of scripture and of sacred tradition.

- The Eastern Orthodox Church principally refers to the Greek Orthodox and Russian Orthodox churches. The Greek Orthodox Church is as old as the Catholic Church.

- The Eastern Orthodox Church gives the most importance to scripture and sacred tradition. It sees the Bible to be both 'infallible' and 'inerrant' (similar to Catholicism and the Baptists). In its tradition, it emphasises apostolic succession, church hierarchy (e.g., priests working under the supervision of Bishops), the early creeds of the Church. Similar to Catholicism. It venerates (treats with great respect) 'saints' in its tradition, who have died for the faith or performed miracles. In this it is similar to Catholicism.

- The Eastern Orthodox Church however, has not embraced Aquinas' thought in the same way as Catholicism has and so does not accept 'natural law theory' and appeals to 'synderesis'.

- The Eastern Orthodox Church maintains ancient practices of worship, unlike Catholicism which updated its liturgy (forms of worship) in the 2nd Vatican Council (1962–5).

- Eastern Orthodoxy accepts the original creeds (traditional statements of Christian belief agreed by the early Church leaders). The Nicene Creed of 325AD claimed that the 'Holy Spirit proceeds from the Father'. In the third Council of Toledo (589AD), the Pope authorised updating this creed, claiming that the 'Holy Spirit proceeds from the Father and the Son'. In Latin, "and the son" is "*filioque*" and so disagreement about this change was called the *filioque* controversy. Rejecting this change, the Eastern Orthodox Church broke away from Catholicism in the "great schism" of 1053. Another reason for this schism was the Eastern Orthodox Churches rejecting the supremacy of the Bishop of Rome, emphasising the authority of a range of Bishops (called "Patriarchs").
- The Eastern Orthodox Church therefore has no supreme authority (similar to the Catholic Pope). Instead, Eastern Orthodox Bishops are 'autocephalous' (self-governing). Collective decisions are coordinated by Patriarchs (authoritative bishops).
- The Eastern Orthodox Church is conservative, having only male bishops and priests and it has not modernised worship as Protestantism did in the 16th c.AD and Catholicism in Vatican 2 (20th c. AD).

> **Mistake to avoid**
>
> Do not confuse the Eastern Orthodox Church with Protestantism. The Eastern Orthodox Church broke from Catholicism in the 'great schism' of 1054 AD. Protestants broke from Catholicism in the 16th century AD.

Sola scriptura (Protestantism)

REVISED ☐

> **Key point**
>
> Protestantism refers to a range of denominations (types of Christian) who broke away from Catholicism in the West in the 16th c. AD. These denominations typically rejected priestly authority in the name of a more direct and personal relationship to God.

- Martin Luther (1483–1546) was a Catholic Augustinian monk, who was outraged by the corruption of the Church. In 1517, he pinned up his "95 theses" for church reform on the door of All Saints' Church, Wittenberg in Germany.
- In particular, Luther denounced the "sale of indulgences" – the church's granting God's forgiveness in return for money as practised by the Dominican friar Johann Tetzel.
- In defending his position against the Church's corrupt practice, Luther appealed to the apostle Paul's idea of 'justification by faith': 'it is clear and certain that this faith alone justifies us.' (*The Smalcald Articles*)
- This inward transformation ('justification') of the person by the power of grace was achieved by God alone. Human institutions like the church, human powers like reason and human ideas of goodness only distracted us from allowing God to transform ('justify') us by the power of His grace.
- To experience this transformational power, we need to read about it in the Bible. We do not need priests to forgive us our sins or thinkers like Aquinas to tell us about the flourishing of nature or about the experience of *synderesis* naturally working within us.

- Luther therefore developed the principle of *'sola scriptura'* – only scripture is authoritative for our coming to know God. He therefore rejects apostolic succession (the institutional authority of the church). In place of a belief in the sacramental power of priests, Luther argued for the 'priesthood of all believers'. Luther also rejected natural law (the authority of reason) and personal experience (as corrupted by the "Fall" described in Genesis 3).

- This principle of seeing only the Bible to be authoritative came to shape most of the Protestant denominations following Luther. For example, the Baptist churches do not have 'ordained' priests with sacramental powers, but 'Ministers' responsible for Bible teaching. They typically reject appeals to 'natural law theory' and our own experiences of goodness.

- The Reformer John Calvin (1509–64) admired Martin Luther, even referring to him as an 'apostle'. Calvin developed a more systematic account of salvation however. He took the process of justification as his starting-point. Individuals could perform no 'works' to be saved. According to Calvin's belief in 'double predestination', God 'predestined' some to salvation and some to damnation. All power lay with God and humans could only act according to God's plan. In asking whether there are going to be 'saved' (i.e., belong to the 'Elect'), humans could only try to discover if they behaved as they are meant to behave – they could not earn a place in heaven by changing their behaviour.

Church of England (Anglicanism).

> **Key point**
>
> Church of England (part of Anglican communion) claims to be both reformed and Catholic, accepting apostolic succession but rejecting the supreme authority of the Pope.

- The Church of England, as well the international Anglican communion it went on to create, adopted a middle position between Catholicism and the Protestants.

- The Church of England maintained a belief in 'apostolic succession' and so the authority of tradition, for which one leader selects the next leader through the power of the Holy Spirit. Nevertheless, it rejected the that one person had supreme authority – i.e., it rejected a belief in the Pope as the only real successor of Peter.

- The King/Queen of England is the ceremonial 'supreme governor of the Church of England' but the Church is practically led by the Archbishops of Canterbury and York and 106 other bishops. The General Synod is an assembly of bishops, clergy and laity who create the laws of the Church.

- The Church of England middle position (*'via media'*) was most clearly articulated by Richard Hooker (1554–79) in his book *Of the Lawes of Ecclesiastical Politie*. Typically shortened to 'Laws', it argues against the *sola scriptura* position, characteristic of Reformed Theology, in favour of our recognising the authority of scripture, tradition, reason and experience similar to Catholicism. At the same time, Hooker rejected the supreme authority of the Bishop of Rome (the Pope).

Quakers (Religious Society of Friends).

REVISED

> **Key point**
> Quakers emphasise 'that of God in every one', identified with the power of love. This experience of God is emphasised instead of scripture, tradition or reason. The Quakers therefore give great importance to individual conscience rather than ordained ministers.

- The Religious Society of Friends, a denomination that is more commonly known as the Quakers, believe in each person's ability to experience the 'light within' and so understand 'that of God in every one'.
- This inner experience of God happens in the heart of the believer through God's grace and is identified with the power of 'love' ('agape').
- This focus on the transformative power of love finds support in scripture, such as Christ's teaching: 'A new commandment I give to you; that you love one another as I have loved you.' (John 13)
- This centrality of love is also supported by Paul's letter to the Corinthians: 'Love never fails. But where there are prophecies, they will cease … these three remain: faith, hope and love. But the greatest of these is love.' (1 Corinthians 13)
- Nevertheless, Quakers do not give great authority to scripture in their worship, typically sitting in silence rather than hearing Bible readings as is common in Catholic, Baptist and Church of England services.
- Quakers also have little church leadership. In 'waiting worship', the congregation sits in a circle, allowing individuals to be inspired by the Holy Spirit each in their own way. No-one conducts sacramental rites (characteristic of Catholicism) or instructs the congregation about the Bible (characteristic of the Baptists).
- There are more "evangelical" forms of Quakers however, who have "programmed" services with a Biblical message from the Pastor and singing. The focus on the 'light within' remains central for such services however.
- The governance of the Quaker Church is open to all and involves listening to God's will rather than debate and argumentation.
- Quakers are Protestants, but they differ significantly from other Protestants (e.g., Baptists). It is therefore best to avoid referring to Protestants as a denomination. Protestantism is a break-away movement from Cathollicism, which includes many denominations.

Recall the definitions ... quiz yourself both ways!

Key word	Definition
Sources of authority	Scripture, tradition, reason & experience
Denomination	Type of Christianity
ROMAN CATHOLICISM	
Largest denomination	Roman Catholicism (1.4 billion) treating scripture, tradition, reason & experience as sources of authority
Pentecost	In Acts 2, the Bible presents the apostles sharing in the power of the Holy Spirit like 'tongues of fire'
Apostolic succession	The Bishops claim to share in the power of the Holy Spirit through being the successors of the apostles, selecting priests to lead God's church.
Clergy	Priests, bishops, etc. who are responsible for leading the church
Ordination	The act of consecrating someone as a priest or Bishop through the power of the Holy Spirit as part of apostolic succession.
Laity	Congregation guided by ordained priests and Bishops
Sacramental powers	Priests claim to share in God's power to heal (Acts 3) and to forgive sins (Matthew 16).
Keys of Peter	Catholicism sees Peter to be the supreme apostle following Matthew 16: 'You are Peter, and upon this rock I will build my church.' The Pope (Bishop of Rome) claims to be the successor of Peter and so now holds Peter's keys to heaven. (Matthew 16)
Pope	Bishop of Rome who is claimed to be the supreme bishop
Nicene Creed	In 325AD, the Christian tradition agreed on the central idea of the 'Trinity' for making sense of the Biblical account of God as Father, Son & Holy Spirit
Council of Rome	Council of Bishops in Rome in 382AD agreed the 'canon' of the Bible.
Ineffabilis Deus	Encyclical of 1854 which makes the teaching of the 'immaculate conception' a requirement of the Catholic faith
Immaculate Conception	Mary, the "mother of God", was born free of original sin
Virgin birth	Jesus was born free or original sin, being fathered by the Holy Spirit rather than by Joseph.
Real presence	God is really present in the eucharist (Mass) and it is not merely a symbol for remembering Jesus's teachings.
Transubstantiation	The bread literally becomes the body of Christ and the wine becomes the blood of Christ in the prayer of consecration
Consecration	The priest prays the words of Jesus sharing his body and blood in the Last Supper, bringing about transubstantiation for Catholics.

Key word	Definition
AQUINAS (CATHOLIC)	
Thomas Aquinas	Pope Leo XIII declared in his encyclical *Aeterni Patris* (1879) that Aquinas' theology was definitive for Catholic doctrine (teaching)
Natural Law Theory	Thomas Aquinas' claim that reason is capable of a functional analysis of things, allowing us to discover their proper function (their God-given purpose)
Synderesis	Aquinas' account of our sense of good and evil that we are born with
Primary precepts	Aquinas' rational principles on how to lead good lives
Secondary precepts	Aquinas' rules on how to lead good lives
2nd Vatican Council	Council of Bishops meeting under the supreme authority of the Pope in 1962-5 modernising Catholic worship and teachings.
EASTERN ORTHODOXY	
2nd largest denomination	Eastern Orthodoxy (220 million) treating scripture & tradition as the sources of authority.
Patriarchs	Influential Bishops coordinating shared decisions by the Eastern Orthodox Church
'autocephalous'	Bishops that are self-governing [not under papal authority]
Great Schism	Eastern Orthodox Church's split from the Catholic Church in 1054AD
Filioque disagreement	The Catholic Church's amending the Nicene Creed to claim that the Holy Spirit proceeds from the Father 'and the Son' (*Filioque*). The Eastern Orthodox Church refused to accept this change.
Council of Toledo	The Catholic Council that agreed to changing the Nicene Creed in 589AD, but the Eastern Orthodox Church did not recognise this.
Papal supremacy	The claim that the Bishop of Rome should have supreme authority as 'Pope', which was one of the reasons for the Great Schism.
PROTESTANTISM	
Protestants	A range of denominations that broke from Catholicism in the 16th century AD over corruption charges
Martin Luther (1483-1546)	Started the Reformation by criticising the sale of indulgences and arguing for *sola scriptura* (the Bible alone is authoritative)
95 theses	Martin Luther's criticisms of Catholicism, posted in 1517
Johann Tetzel	Dominican Friar who was very successful in selling indulgences
Sola scriptura	Scripture alone should be the source of authority (Martin Luther)
Smalcald Articles	Luther's prioritising 'justification by faith' against 'justification by works' (i.e., requirements of the Catholic priesthood)
Individual conscience	Martin Luther rejected the sacramental power of priests to forgive sins, arguing instead for personal confession.
Priesthood of all believers	Martin Luther rejected church hierarchy (e.g., the Pope) in favour of congregations having responsibility for their own spiritual growth.
John Calvin	Protestant Reformer who argued that the sovereign power of God leads to double predestination – people's after life in heaven or hell is decided by God and not by our actions.

Key word	Definition
	ANGLICANISM (to which Church of England belongs)
3rd largest denominations	Anglicanism (110 million) treat scripture, tradition, reason & authority as authoritative following Richard Hooker
Hooker	Richard Hooker (1554-79) was a significant Anglican theologian arguing for the importance of scripture, tradition, reason & experience.
Church structure	Similar to Eastern Orthodoxy, the Church of England accepts apostolic succession, but rejects Papal authority. The Church of England's Bishops are more progressive than Eastern Orthodox ones however.
	BAPTISTS
4th largest denomination	Baptists (100 million)
Baptists	Evangelical Christians who are concerned to share the 'good news' of the Bible's teachings. They follow Martin Luther in focusing on the priesthood of all believers against traditional ordained clergy. They also accept the 'sola scriptura' principle and so the supreme authority of the Bible.
	QUAKERS
5th largest denomination	Quakers (0.4 million)
Individual conscience	Emphasises inner experience of God, often through practices of meditation (silent sitting). In this way, we experience 'that of God in every one.' No ordained clergy is required for this.
John 13	'A new commandment I give to you; that you love one another as I have loved you.'
1 Corinthians 13	these three remain: faith, hope and love. But the greatest of these is love.'

Test yourself

(a) Outline **two** forms of authority in any one Christian denomination. (4)
(b) Explain the role of individual conscience in matters of belief and practice. (6)
(c) "An ordained ministry is needed to lead the laity."
Discuss this statement considering the arguments for and against.
  In your answer you should include:
  - reference to teachings
  - other (divergent) points of view – either within the religion or from other religions
  - your opinion/point of view using reasoned arguments
  - a balanced conclusion. (10)

2.1.2 Founders & Leaders

GENERIC SYLLABUS REQUIREMENTS
The life of the religion's founder(s) as a role model for believers, including the founder's status & importance in that religion. The significance of the founder's teachings for how religious believers live, including examples to illustrate this. The importance of other historical and contemporary leaders in the religion.

CHRISTIAN SYLLABUS REQUIREMENTS
Jesus Christ's life, and in particular his baptism, temptations, crucifixion & resurrection; two accounts of his healing ministry; Jesus' account of discipleship; and his importance for Christians today.

Jesus as the 'new covenant'

> **Key point**
>
> Jesus is seen to be the promised Messiah, fulfilling the covenants of the Old Testament.

- The Old Testament speaks of a number of 'covenants' between God and His people.
- These covenants involve commitments by God, which at times require commitments from humans in return. The Hebrew word for covenant is '*berit*', which is "an agreement enacted between two parties in which one or both make promises under oath."
- The Old Testament includes a series of covenants:

  1. **Covenant to Noah of Genesis 9**: God promises to all life that He will no longer destroy the world by flood, marking this with a rainbow.
  2. **Covenant to Abraham of Genesis 12-17**: God blesses Abraham with many descendants (the Jews, marked out by circumcision) and a 'promised land'.
  3. **Covenant to Moses of Exodus**: God gives the Jews his holy law, including the 10 commandments of Exodus 20; humans are required to live according to God's law.
  4. **Davidic covenant (2 Samuel 7)**: Even under the law, the people of God fail to live a godly life and God promises them an 'anointed' leader (one ritually marked out with sacred oils). This is in Hebrew the promised 'Messiah'.

- The New Testament is the fulfilment of those covenants:

  5. **New Covenant**: in Jesus we experience the life of God, fulfilling the previous relationships to God (covenants). This relationship to God is more complete than previous relationships, with God sacrificing his supreme power so as to empower us through the power of His love.

Jesus as the incarnation

> **Key point**
>
> Jesus is God on earth as the character of God is revealed in the character of this human.

- God is referred to in the Bible as Father, Son and Holy Spirit. In making sense of this, the Church decided that God was 'Trinity' – 'three persons of one substance' as formulated in the Nicene Creed of 325AD.
- God the Son is the 'word' or understanding, who exists eternally with the Father (the source of existence). The Son or word was then 'incarnated' as Jesus.
- God therefore 'became flesh' as a human being, revealing the character of God in the character of a human.
- Jesus is therefore claimed to be 'fully human and fully God – we experience the character of God in the character of this human.
- Jesus was conceived by 'virgin birth' with the human Mary as his mother and God as his father. (Luke 2)
- Original sin is the sin all humanity shares in after the 'first sin' of Adam and Eve eating from the 'tree of the knowledge of good and evil' in the Garden of Eden. (Genesis 4) All human nature is claimed to become selfish by this act, judging things in terms of what is good for oneself rather than truly good. Jesus' 'virgin birth' means that he is born free of 'original sin' and so cares for what is truly good rather than what is merely good for him. (As discussed above, Catholic theology claims that Mary has also been born free or original sin by her 'immaculate conception'.)

Jesus's baptism by John

> **Key point**
>
> Baptism is originally John the Baptist's ritual of washing people free of sin. Jesus undergoes baptism and afterwards the three 'persons' of the Trinity are seen together for the first time.

- John was Jesus' cousin, wearing clothes of camel's hair, living on locusts and wild honey, demanding modesty and self-examination.
- He preached to the Jews that they needed to not simply change how they behave – e.g., following the 613 rules of Judaism is not enough. They also needed to change who they are – live a more godly life.
- John did this by requiring people to wash themselves free of sin in the River Jordan so as to live a godly life. This ritual came to be called the 'baptism' of repentance (saying sorry for how one has lived and asking God to make one a better person).
- John proclaims that another will come after him who will not baptise with water, but with the Holy Spirit. This is Jesus.

- Jesus comes to John to be baptised and he says, 'I need to be baptised by you, and do you come to me?' (Matthew 3) This is because Jesus is born free of original sin and so does not need to be washed of that sin.

- Jesus replies, 'it is proper for us to do this to fulfil all righteousness.' (Matthew 3) The Church traditionally interprets Jesus' reply to mean that he is performing this ritual so that his followers will do it – not to wash himself free of sin.

- Matthew 3 goes on to claim: 'As soon as Jesus was baptised, he went up out of the water. At that moment heaven was opened, and he saw the Spirit of God descending like a dove and alighting on him. And a voice from heaven said, 'This is my Son, whom I love; with him I am well pleased.' All 'persons' of the Trinity are therefore claimed to be present at Jesus' baptism. God the Father is the voice from heaven. God the Son (the eternal 'word' or *logos*) is incarnated as Jesus. God the Holy Spirit is present as a dove.

> **Mistake to avoid**
>
> Jesus' baptism does not directly refer to the Trinity. Indeed, the Bible does not itself use the word 'Trinity'. The baptism scene does describe God as Father, Son and Holy Spirit. In trying to make sense of these three names of God, the Church agreed upon the idea of the Trinity: 'three persons of one substance' or nature [Nicene Creed of 325AD]

- Baptism becomes one of the central rites (rituals) of the church and a sacrament for the Catholic, Eastern Orthodox and Anglican churches. Indeed, Jesus himself requires it in his 'great commission': 'All authority in heaven and on earth has been given to me. Therefore go and make disciples of all nations, baptizing them in the name of the Father and of the Son and of the Holy Spirit.' (Matthew 28)

Jesus' temptations   REVISED

> **Key point**
>
> After being baptised, Jesus goes up a mountain to fast and is tempted three times by the devil. Having resisted these temptations, Jesus' ministry of healing & teaching begins.

- The synoptic Gospels of Matthew, Mark & Luke all present Jesus' temptation by the devil following his baptism by John.

- Mark's account of the temptations is very short and includes just the following: 'At once the Spirit sent him out into the wilderness, and he was in the wilderness for forty days, being tempted by Satan. He was with the wild animals, and angels attended him.' (Mark 1)

- The accounts of the temptations in Matthew's and Luke's Gospels are more detailed and include a conversation between Jesus and the devil. The conversations are almost identical in wording in both Gospels. 'Source Critics' (see above) have used this as evidence that Matthew and Luke both used a lost source 'Q' when describing Jesus' temptations since this explains their almost identical wording.

- The conversations involve three temptations. Matthew and Luke put the temptations in slightly different orders in spite of their using the same words in each temptation. We shall follow the order of Luke's Gospel here.
  1. **Greed**: ''If you are the Son of God, tell this stone to become bread.' In spite of being hungry from his fast, Jesus quotes scripture in response to the devil, saying: 'It is written: "Man shall not live on bread alone."'
  2. **Power**: In the 2nd temptation, the devil promises Jesus limitless power, represented by 'the kingdoms of the world. Jesus again responds by quoting scripture, saying: 'It is written: "Worship the Lord your God and serve him only."'
  3. **Vanity**: In the 3rd temptation, the devil dares Jesus to throw himself off from the highest point of the temple, while quoting scripture's claim that angels will protect him "so that you will not strike your foot against a stone." Jesus quotes scripture back at the devil: ''It is said: "Do not put the Lord your God to the test."' (Luke 4)
- Matthew 4 gives a very similar account of the temptations, but orders them differently, tempting Jesus firstly with greed, then vanity and finally power.
- In all three synoptic Gospels however, Jesus successfully resists temptation and begins his ministry of healing and teaching.

Miracles

> **Key point**
>
> Conservatives interpret miracles literally whereas liberals interpret miracles symbolically. We shall discuss physical and mental healing (exorcisms).

- The term 'miracle' ('*dunamis*' in Greek) concerns the power of God.
- Miracles are typically divided into 4 groups:
  1. miracles of physical healing
  2. miracles of psychological healing (exorcism)
  3. miracles regarding nature (e.g., Jesus' calming the storm or walking on water)
  4. the miracle of the resurrection.
- The syllabus requires students to know two examples of Jesus' ministry of miraculous healing.
- For conservative Christians (and most Muslims), the miracles of Jesus literally occurred. These are presented in the Old Testament – e.g., the parting of the Red Sea by Moses in Exodus 14. Miracles are also present in the New Testament, performed both by Jesus and by his apostles – e.g., Jesus says before his ascension to heaven, 'And these signs will accompany those who believe: In my name they will drive out demons; they will speak in new tongues; they will pick up snakes with their hands; and when they drink deadly poison, it will not hurt them at all; they will place their hands on sick people, and they will get well." (Mark 16)

- The sceptical philosopher David Hume (1711-76) in his *Enquiries Concerning Human Understanding* argued that miracles involved a violation of the laws of nature'. Further, he claimed, 'No testimony is sufficient to establish a miracle, unless the testimony be of such a kind, that its falsehood would be more miraculous.' In other words, we should accept the more likely explanation and not appeal to supernatural powers unless there is good reason to.

- James Keller (1900-77) in his *Moral Argument Against Miracles* writes: 'The claim that God has worked a miracle implies that God has singled out certain persons for some benefit which many others do not receive implies that God is unfair. 'For liberal Christians, influenced by historical criticism (see '2.1.1a; *Modern Interpretations of the Bible* above), they read the stories as not literally true. Indeed, the liberal Christian theologian Rudolf Bultmann (1884-1976) argues: 'It is impossible to use electric light and the wireless and to avail ourselves of modern medical and surgical discoveries, and at the same time to believe in the New Testament world of spirits and miracles.'

- Rudolf Bultmann even accepts that the Biblical authors were themselves not clear on the distinction between real causal powers and fictional magical (miraculous) powers.

- Nevertheless Bultmann continued to believe in the symbolic importance of the miracles. He therefore argued that we had to 'demythologise' the Bible so as to no longer read the miracles as literally true but as spiritually true – teaching us not about supernatural powers but about life's meaning, how we should live and what we should hope for.

- The American Anglican bishop John Shelby Spong (1931-) in his book *Jesus for the Non Religious*, similarly argues that miracles highlight Jesus' teachings about what it means to be truly human, and not what it means to be super-human.

> **Mistake to avoid**
>
> It is not the case that conservative Christians believe in literal interpretations of miracles and liberal Christians believe in symbolic interpretations. Rather, conservative Christians believe in *both* literal and symbolic interpretations of miracles. Liberal Christians reject literal interpretations for scientific reasons, but agree with symbolic interpretations.

Jesus miraculously heals a blind man (John 9)

REVISED ☐

> **Key point**
>
> On Conservative readings of scripture, this story demonstrates Jesus' supernatural powers of healing someone blind at birth, demonstrating that Jesus is the Son of God. On a liberal interpretation of scripture, this story makes clear what it means to believe in the life of God revealed in Jesus – not judging others based on scripture, but living out the purposes of God revealed in scripture.

Jesus Heals a Man Born Blind

As he went along, he saw a man blind from birth. His disciples asked him, "Rabbi, who sinned, this man or his parents, that he was born blind?"
"Neither this man nor his parents sinned," said Jesus, "but this happened so that the works of God might be displayed in him. As long as it is day, we must do the works of him who sent me. Night is coming, when no one can work. While I am in the world, I am the light of the world."
After saying this, he spit on the ground, made some mud with the saliva, and put it on the man's eyes. "Go," he told him, "wash in the Pool of Siloam" (this word means "Sent"). So the man went and washed, and came home seeing. […]
They brought to the Pharisees the man who had been blind. Now the day on which Jesus had made the mud and opened the man's eyes was a Sabbath. Therefore the Pharisees also asked him how he had received his sight. "He put mud on my eyes," the man replied, "and I washed, and now I see."
Some of the Pharisees said, "This man is not from God, for he does not keep the Sabbath." […]
The [healed] man answered, "Now that is remarkable! You don't know where he [Jesus] comes from, yet he opened my eyes. We know that God does not listen to sinners. He listens to the godly person who does his will. Nobody has ever heard of opening the eyes of a man born blind. If this man were not from God, he could do nothing."
To this they [the Pharisees] replied, "You were steeped in sin at birth; how dare you lecture us!" And they threw him out. […]
Jesus heard that they had thrown him out, and when he found him, he said, "Do you believe in the Son of Man?"
"Who is he, sir?" the man asked. "Tell me so that I may believe in him."
Jesus said, "You have now seen him; in fact, he is the one speaking with you."
Then the man said, "Lord, I believe," and he worshiped him.
Jesus said, "For judgment I have come into this world, so that the blind will see and those who see will become blind."
Some Pharisees who were with him heard him say this and asked, "What? Are we blind too?"
Jesus said, "If you were blind, you would not be guilty of sin; but now that you claim you can see, your guilt remains.
(John 9)

IGCSE 2 Religious Studies

ANALYSIS OF JOHN 9

- Jesus' healing the blind man is an example of a physical healing miracle.
- The disciples ask Jesus whose sin was the cause of the blindness. This is reasonable since Jesus often equates physical healing with spiritual healing. For example on healing a paralytic, Jesus asks: 'Which is easier: to say, "Your sins are forgiven," or to say, "Get up and walk"?' (Matthew 9) The disciples are therefore asking whose sin caused the blindness – the person himself or his parents.
- Jesus responds that sin is not the cause of the blindness; rather than looking for its cause, Jesus treats the blindness/sin as an opportunity for his doing good.
- To heal the man born blind from birth, Jesus applied mud made from the ground mixed with his own saliva to the man's eyes.
- The man is washed in the pool meaning 'sent' (Siloam) and regains his sight.
- The Pharisees (Jews concerned with textual obedience) note that Jesus is healing this man on the Sabbath; this is this holy day of rest, the 4th of the 10 commandments, given to the Jews by the prophet Moses (Exodus 20).
- Using the law to judge him, the Pharisees try to persuade the healed man to condemn Jesus as a 'sinner' who is not from God. The healed man replies that Jesus has 'opened my eyes', arguing that 'if this man were not from God, he could do nothing.'
- The Pharisees then attack the healed man for being a sinner and throw him out.
- Jesus finds the healed man, asking him, 'Do you believe in the Son of Man?' The healed man replies, 'Who is he, sir?' Jesus replies, 'You have now seen him; in fact, he is the one speaking with you.' The healed man replies, 'Lord, I believe'. This suggests that the purpose of the miracle is for Jesus to reveal the life of God in himself
- Finally, the passage returns to the question of the cause of blindness. Jesus says to the healed man, 'I have come into this world, so that the blind will see and those who see will become blind.'
- The Pharisees sense that they are being attacked and ask, 'What? Are we blind too?'
- Jesus responds: 'If you were blind, you would not be guilty of sin; but now that you claim you can see, your guilt remains.' This therefore involves a reversal of the beginning of the miracle story – the blind man is now the innocent person and those who sit in judgment on him (believing that they can see God's requirements for others) are the sinners.
- The miracle story therefore reflects on how to interpret scripture. The Pharisees use scripture to judge others – what we might call a 'juridical' or legalistic interpretation of scripture. Jesus sees scripture to reveal God's purposes, which he tries to share in – what Albert Schweitzer (1875-1965) in his book *Quest for the Historical Jesus* called an 'eschatological' interpretation of scripture, where *eschaton* refers to the end time or purpose of history

INTERPRETATION OF JOHN 9

- On a literal interpretation, the story is factual; Jesus actually healed a person of blindness from birth by spitting on the earth to create mud, applying this to his eyes and then having him wash this mud off in the Pool of Siloam.

- On a symbolic interpretation, the story is theological; the interpretation is focused not on the facts, but on how to understand God. On this interpretation, the miracle is rejecting the Pharisees' juridical (legalistic) understanding of God, characterised in terms of judging others on the basis of the God's laws (e.g., whether they have obeyed the commandment of not working on the Sabbath). The miracle story is supporting Jesus' eschatological understanding of scripture, characterised in terms of our coming to see and share in the purposes of God (i.e., our working to achieve the 'kingdom of God on earth as it is in heaven'). In other words, the miracle story is claiming that the life of God is not in service to the law; the law is in service to revealing the life (purposes) of God.

- Conservative readings of this miracle accept *both* the literal and the symbolic interpretations as true. Liberal readings of the miracle reject its literal interpretation as untrue (characteristic of an unscientific age), but see its spiritual message to be true.

Jesus' healing of the bleeding woman (Mark 5)

REVISED

> **Key point**
>
> Jesus' healing of the woman challenges juridical understandings of purity in favour of eschatological understandings of purification.

> **Jesus heals the bleeding woman**
>
> 'And a woman was there who had been subject to bleeding for twelve years. She had suffered a great deal under the care of many doctors and had spent all she had, yet instead of getting better she grew worse. When she heard about Jesus, she came up behind him in the crowd and touched his cloak, because she thought, "If I just touch his clothes, I will be healed." Immediately her bleeding stopped and she felt in her body that she was freed from her suffering. At once Jesus realized that power had gone out from him. He turned around in the crowd and asked, "Who touched my clothes?" "You see the people crowding against you," his disciples answered, "and yet you can ask, 'Who touched me?'" "But Jesus kept looking around to see who had done it. Then the woman, knowing what had happened to her, came and fell at his feet and, trembling with fear, told him the whole truth. He said to her, "Daughter, your faith has healed you. Go in peace and be freed from your suffering."'
> (Mark 5:1-20)

ANALYSIS OF MARK 5

- This story appears in all three synoptic Gospels: Matthew gives the shortest narrative, and his account includes some differences (e.g., the woman is healed after speaking to Jesus rather than touching his cloak). Luke's Gospel includes some identical sections to Mark's Gospel supporting the two-documentary hypothesis (see Biblical interpretation above).

- The story of the miraculous healing of the woman with the 'issue of blood' is sandwiched in the Bible's account of another miraculous healing: Jesus' raising of Jairus' daughter from death. This stylistic element of introducing a story within a story is called by Biblical scholars an intercalated narrative.

IGCSE 2 Religious Studies

- Under Jewish law, a 'niddah' or menstruating woman is judged to be unclean and the bleeding would have had to have stopped for 7 days to be pure again. Given her medical condition, the woman with the issue of blood would be in a continual state of impurity.
- This state of impurity would have resulted in social and religious isolation.
- Because of the continual bleeding, the woman would have been continually regarded in Jewish law as a "niddah" or menstruating woman, and so ceremonially unclean. In order to be regarded as clean, the flow of blood would need to stop for at least 7 days. Because of the constant bleeding, this woman lived in a continual state of uncleanness which would have brought upon her social and religious isolation.
- Jesus senses that some power has left him, and the woman who touched his cloak confesses.
- Jesus is not angry, but congratulates the woman for sharing in his power: 'Daughter, your faith has healed you. Go in peace and be freed from your suffering.'

INTERPRETATION OF MARK 5

- On a literal interpretation, this story is communicating a factual message: Jesus has supernatural powers that others can share in through touching Jesus' clothing, and so be healed of medical conditions (i.e., an "issue of blood").
- Interpreted symbolically, the miracle is challenging Jewish understandings of salvation. For the Pharisees, salvation is understood in terms of purity, identified with obedience to God's law. The menstruating woman, who is judged to be impure, therefore needs to be regulated before she can be admitted back into a state of purity.
- For Jesus, salvation is not understood in terms of purity. Rather, purity is understood in terms of the power of salvation. By sharing in that power of salvation, we are purified.
- Jesus "incarnates" that power, and others (such as the woman with an "issue of bood") can share in that power through him and be healed.
- The miracle therefore symbolically presents a new understanding of salvation. We should not understand salvation in terms of laws about who is and who is not pure. We should rather understand salvation in terms of sharing in the transformative purpose of history – what Christians call the "will of God".
- Conservative readings of this miracle accept *both* the literal and the symbolic interpretations as true. Liberal readings of the miracle reject its literal interpretation (as unscientific), but see its spiritual message to be true.

Jesus' teaching about discipleship: Sermon on the Mount `REVISED`

> **Key point**
>
> Jesus' teaching about discipleship is focused on sharing in the purposes of God instead of judging people in terms of God's law. Our discussion will focus on Jesus' Sermon on the Mount in Matthew 5–7 since Matthew gathers together all of Jesus' teachings together in this section.

- In the Synoptic Gospels of Matthew, Mark and Luke, Jesus teaches about discipleship through parables – stories about the importance of sharing in God's purposes and bringing about 'kingdom of God on earth as it is in heaven'. In John's Gospel, Jesus teaches about discipleship through the "I am" sayings – we learn how to share in God's purposes through the life of Jesus. Nevertheless, all of the Gospels give a consistent account of Jesus' teaching about discipleship – it involves sharing oneself in God's purposes rather than judging others in terms of God's law.
- Matthew's Gospel gathers Jesus' teachings about discipleship together, presenting most of them in the Sermon on the Mount (Matthew 5–7). This sermon is the first of the Five Discourses of Matthew. This first 'discourse' occurs early in Jesus' ministry in Galilee, after he has been baptised by John the Baptist and then tempted by the devil. It is the longest continuous discourse of Jesus found in the New Testament, most systematically presenting Jesus' approach to discipleship.
- The Sermon can be divided into 3 main sections:
  1. Beatitudes (blessings) – rather than focusing on laws, Jesus focuses on the qualities or attitudes that his disciples need to have. (Matthew 5: 3–12).
  2. The Antitheses – Jesus challenges Judaism's traditional focus on the law in favour of his new focus on the purpose that law serves – what he calls the 'kingdom of God on earth as it is in heaven.' He introduces this challenge in terms of a series of antitheses: 'You have heard it said … But I say to you …' (Matthew 5:17–48)
  3. True discipleship: Jesus discusses the righteousness necessary to enter the 'narrow gateway' to achieve God's purposes, which is only possible by 'building on solid foundations'. (Matthew 6–7)
- Luke gives a shorter account of these teachings in the 'Sermon on the Plain' (Luke 6).

Sermon on the Mount 1: the Beatitudes `REVISED`

> **Key point**
>
> Beatitudes means blessings and focuses on the blessed characteristics required for true discipleship. (Matthew 5: 3–12)

- The word *beatitude* comes from the Latin *beatitudo*, meaning "blessedness." There are 8 'beatitudes' or characteristics that are blessings from God.
- The 8 beatitudes are typically divided into three main sections:

1. Beatitudes 1-3 focus on the need for God.
2. Beatitudes 4-7 focus on the search for God or life's purpose.
3. Beatitude 8 focuses on the resilience required for fulfilling's life's (God's) purpose, claiming that this state involves real happiness. The last two sections concern how the disciples can embody these virtues by being resilient.

- The Beatitudes are as follows:
  1. Beatitudes 1-3 require disciples to recognise their real needs since they will then act on behalf of what is really necessary (God's will) rather than their own selfishness.
      1. *Blessed are the poor in spirit, for theirs is the Kingdom of Heaven.*
      2. *Blessed are those who mourn, for they will be comforted.*
      3. *Blessed are the meek, for they will inherit the Earth.*
- Beatitudes 4-7 focus on the search for God or life's purpose.
    4. *Blessed are those who hunger and thirst for righteousness, for they will be satisfied*
    5. *Blessed are the merciful, for they will be shown mercy.*
    6. *Blessed are the pure in heart, for they will see God.*
    7. *Blessed are the peacemakers, for they will be called children of God.*
- Beatitude 8 focuses on the resilience required for fulfilling's life's (God's) purpose, claiming that this state involves real happiness.
    8. *Blessed are those who are persecuted because of righteousness, for theirs is the Kingdom of Heaven.*
- The last claims are qualities the disciples must have if they are to share in these blessed characteristics or virtues. The 9th blessed is not therefore traditionally treated as a distinct 'beatitude', but characteristics necessary for achieving the state of beatitude.
    - *Blessed are you when people insult you, persecute you and falsely say all kinds of evil against you because of me.*
    - *Rejoice and be glad, because great is your reward in heaven, for in the same way they persecuted the prophets who were before you.*

Sermon on the Mount 2: the Antitheses   REVISED

> **Key point**
>
> In the Antitheses, Jesus challenges traditional Judaism's focus on obedience to the law of God in favour of his own focus the 'spirit' or purpose of that law. Jesus' teachings seem to be the 'antitheses' (contradictions) of Old Testament law, but claim to be the fulfilment of that law.

- In the Antitheses, Jesus challenges traditional interpretations of the law by focusing less on the need to submit to the law and more on living according to the Spirit or purpose of the law.
- Jesus states, 'You have heard it said ...' and then quotes some of the Mosaic law (i.e., the laws of the Old Testament's *Torah* that were traditionally claimed to be revealed to

Moses – there are 613 such rules). He then challenges each claim, stating, 'but I say to you ...'. These challenges are called the 'antitheses', since Jesus seems to be contradicting the Old Testament law. As Robert Gundry argues in his *Commentary of Matthew* however, Jesus is not aiming to contradict the law, but to interpret it in the light of 'the goal toward which it was already headed'. Gundry even suggests renaming the 'Antitheses' the 'Culminations' so as to avoid this misinterpretation.

- Before the Antitheses, Jesus makes it clear that he has not come to 'abolish' the law but to 'fulfil it'. He even declares the law to be valid until 'Heaven and Earth pass away' and 'all things are accomplished'. He even directly identifies righteousness with the law itself, but he also talks of a 'greater righteousness', which is required 'to enter the kingdom of God' (i.e., share in the fulfilment of God's law).

- The 6 antitheses are tabulated below as follows: in the left column is what is commanded in the Old Testament, which Jesus introduces with the words, 'You have heard it said ...'. In the right column, is Jesus' interpretation of this commandment in terms of what someone should live for and so who they should be.

'You have heard that it was said ...'	'But I say to you ...'
'Do not murder' (Exodus 20)	Purify yourself of anger or you will be judged for your character.
'Do not commit adultery' (Exodus 20)	Purify yourself of lust to avoid hell.
'Anyone who divorces his wife must give her a certificate of divorce' (Deuteronomy 24)	Be faithful in marriage; unfaithfulness is adultery.
'Do not break your oath, but keep the oaths you have made to the Lord.'	'Do not swear (i.e., make oaths) at all.' …. 'Simply let your "Yes" be "Yes," and your "No," "No".'
'Eye for eye, and tooth for tooth.' (Exodus 21)	'Do not resist an evil person. If someone strikes you on the right cheek, turn to him the other also'.
'Love your neighbour' (Leviticus 19)	'Love your enemies and pray for those who persecute you'.

- We can therefore summarise the 6 antitheses as follows
  1. The purpose of the commandment to not murder is to live at peace.
  2. The purpose of the prohibition of adultery is to purify oneself of lust.
  3. The purpose of the rules on divorce are to encourage faithfulness.
  4. The purpose of the rules on oaths is to be responsible.
  5. The purpose of the *lex talionis* (eye for an eye rule) is to achieve fairness, which can only be achieved through forgiveness.
  6. The purpose of loving one's neighbour is to love all of God's creation – not just one's allies.

- The chapter ends by encouraging his disciples to seek after perfection (*teleios* in Greek) meaning 'full maturity' of character. This is the requirement of 'greater righteousness'.

Sermon on the Mount 3: true discipleship

> **Key point**
>
> The 3rd section of the Sermon on the Mount focuses on the how true disciples should behave. They should live simple, self-critical lives focused on achieving God's purposes and not stand in judgment on others or try to present an image of themselves to others.

- Having discussed the character of discipleship in the Beatitudes (characterised by openness to God), and the proper attitude to the law in the Antitheses (characterised by identifying with the purposes of God), Jesus now goes on to discuss the behaviour of discipleship.
- Jesus rejects outward acts of religious obedience so as to present the image of righteousness to others. Fasting and charity should therefore not be advertised, but should be done simply and privately. In this way, people please God rather than themselves.
- Jesus rejects complex prayers that show how religious someone is in favour of straightforward prayers that show how faithful someone is.
- Jesus gives an example of simple, heartfelt prayer in his Lord's prayer: 'Our Father in heaven, hallowed be your name, your kingdom come, your will be done, on earth as in heaven. Give us today our daily bread. Forgive us our sins as we forgive those who sin against us. Lead us not into temptation but deliver us from evil. For the kingdom, the power, and the glory are yours now and for ever. Amen.'
- Jesus claims the true disciple should not be concerned with worldly wealth but with the spiritual 'treasures' that cannot be destroyed. Jesus presents us with a choice between worshipping wealth and God.
- Jesus claims that the true disciple does not stand in judgment on others; the true disciple is rather concerned to become closer to God and to live for God's purposes (the 'kingdom of God').
- Jesus uses the image of a narrow gateway to make sense of the path of righteousness he is calling us to share in. The broad, easy pathway of selfishness is claimed to lead to destruction. The path of discipleship is difficult, by contrast, and yet it offers eternal rewards – the fulfilment of God's kingdom.
- In the final section, Jesus claims that just as a house built on sand is washed away, a faith without secure foundations is destroyed. True righteousness has deep foundations, and these are to be found in sharing in the 'will of God' or the purposes of God.

Jesus' crucifixion

> **Key point**
>
> Jesus' crucifixion is at the heart of all 4 Gospels. The death of the innocent man Jesus highlights the injustice of our world and Jesus' forgiveness breaks the cycle of violence and allows for the atonement for sin, reconciling us with God.

- Crucifixion is method of punishment practised by the ancient Romans in which the convicted person was tied to a large wooden cross and left to hang there until exhaustion and asphyxiation (incapacity to breathe due to the weight of the body) kills the person.
- Crucifixion was reserved for more serious crimes due to the humiliation of the person's hanging helplessly on the cross and due to the extreme pain it caused before death.
- The crucifixion of Jesus is described in all four Gospels and to secure this punishment, the Jewish authorities had to appeal to the Roman Governor of the Province of Judaea, Pontius Pilate (who served in this role from 26/7AD to 36/7AD).
- During a Jewish celebration of *Pesach* or the Passover (which remembers the angel of death passing over the Jewish families as it killed the Egyptian first born sons for enslaving the Jews), Jesus created the ritual of 'communion', claiming that in sharing the bread and the wine the disciples are sharing in Jesus' body and blood (i.e., the life of God).
- Jesus then goes to pray in the Garden of Gethsemane, knowing that he is to be killed, and prays: 'Father, if you are willing, take this cup from me; yet not my will, but yours be done.' (Luke 22) It is God's will however. The apostle Judas had betrayed Jesus for 30 pieces of silver so the Jewish leaders were able to arrest Jesus. Jesus tells Peter not to fight when he is arrested, even healing the soldier whom Paul had injured on the ear.
- The soldiers take Jesus to the Jewish leader Herod Antipas (popularly known as King Herod), who mocks Jesus for claiming to be king of the Jews. Herod then sends Jesus to Ponitus Pilate (the Roman governor) for trial.
- Pontius Pilate tries to avoid executing Jesus, seeing him to be innocent, but the Jewish crowds insist that Jesus should be crucified. Pilate agrees to this so as to keep the peace.
- Jesus is flogged, condemned to death, and forced to carry the cross on which he was to be executed to the 'Place of a Skull' (Golgotha). Jesus was charged with claiming to be 'King of the Jews' and so a threat to Roman rule: this charge was written on the cross. The soldiers encounter Simon of Cyrene and force him to help Jesus carry the cross.
- Jesus was crucified and hung between two convicted thieves. One of the thieves cursed and mocked Jesus, but the other thief admitted his guilt and saw no guilt in Jesus.
- Jesus dies asking God to forgive those who had sentenced him to death.
- At Jesus' death, Mark's Gospel claims that the sun went dark for 3 hours whereas Matthew's Gospel claimed that there was an earthquake. Roman soldiers thrust a spear in Jesus' side to ensure he was dead before taking him down from the cross.

- The crucifixion is interpreted as a sacrifice for sin; such sacrifices were common in ancient times. In the Bible, Abraham almost sacrifices his son Isaac as a sign of his commitment to God, but God does not require it. (Genesis 22) Another important sacrifice is the sacrifice of the lamb celebrated in the Passover, whose blood was placed on the doors of the Jews so that the angel of death passed over their families and so only killed the first born of the Egyptians. (Exodus 12) Jesus' sacrifice is distinct however; Jesus sacrifices himself so as to expose the sin of the world and his forgiveness cures it.
- The crucifixion of Jesus is meant to act as an atonement for sin – it makes all humanity at-one with God by highlighting that sin and also pointing beyond that sin through the power of God's forgiveness revealed in Christ.

Jesus' resurrection

REVISED

> **Key point**
>
> Jesus' resurrection is literally his coming back from the dead, but theologically it is the overcoming of sin and death. It is the 'particular resurrection' that prefigures the 'general resurrection' of all coming back from the dead at the second coming ('*Parousia*') of Christ at the end time ('*eschaton*').

- With Jesus' crucifixion, the incarnation of God (the life of God revealed in Christ) dies. As such, the life of 'faith, hope and love' (1 Corinthians 13) dies.
- Jesus is taken down from the cross and is laid in a tomb cut in the rock given to him by Joseph of Arimathea. Joseph has him wrapped in linen and the tomb is sealed with a large rock.
- On the third day, Jesus rises from the dead. Mary Magdalene comes to the tomb and finds the stone moved away. Angels announce that Jesus has risen from the dead and Jesus appears to Mary Magdalene although she does not recognise him at first.
- Jesus also appears to the apostles, although again they do not immediately recognise Jesus. Jesus breaks bread with the disciples and eats fish with them on the shore.
- Jesus is claimed to come back to life as an 'imperishable' 'spiritual body' rather than a 'perishable' 'natural body'. This resurrection body is claimed to be of heaven in contrast to the natural body which is of the earth. (1 Corinthians 15)
- Having conquered sin and death with the resurrection, Jesus does not die, but his heavenly body returns to heaven, 40 days after the resurrection.
- This afterlife is promised to all who share in the life of God revealed in Christ: 'Christ has indeed been raised from the dead, the first fruits of those who have fallen asleep.' (1 Corinthians 15)

- Jesus' own resurrection is termed the 'particular resurrection' and points towards the 'general resurrection' at Jesus' 'second coming' ('*parousia*') when all people will rise from the dead at the end time ('*eschaton*') and gain 'resurrection bodies'. Those who are judged to share in the life of God belong to the 'new creation'.
- Conservative Christians like N.T. Wright interpret the resurrection literally – it is factually accurate that Jesus rose from the dead and we shall all rise from the dead at the end time and gain resurrection bodies.
- Liberal Christians like Marcus Borg interpret the resurrection symbolically: 'The truth of Easter (the resurrection) really has nothing to do with whether the tomb was empty on a particular morning 2,000 years ago or whether anything happened to the corpse of Jesus. I see the truth of Easter as grounded in the Christian experience of Jesus as a living spiritual reality of the present.' In other words, the resurrection is the expression of a life of 'faith, hope and love' – it is not a factual description.

Jesus' significance for Christians today

> **Key point**
>
> For Conservative Christians, Jesus' significance lies in his miraculous power to save us from sin; no other figure in history has that power. For Liberal Christians, Jesus' significance is that of a teacher of wisdom, showing us how to live with 'faith, hope and love'. Other figures in history (e.g., Buddha) might teach the same thing in a different way.

INCARNATION

- Jesus' significance is that of the incarnation – the eternal Son or word of God is incarnated as a human (John 1). Jesus is fully human and fully God, allowing us to know the character of God and so share in the Beatitudes (blessed characteristics of God). This allows us to go beyond obedience to God to sharing in the life of God. St Paul in his letters to both the Romans and Galatians explains this in terms of 'justification by works' (works of obedience to the law that make us just) and 'justification by faith' (a life of faith that share in God's life of justice).

MIRACULOUS POWERS

- For conservative Christians, Jesus has the significance of a miracle worker, who has the power to cure people of illness, exorcise demons (e.g., cure the possessed man Legion in Mark 5 & Luke 8), raise people from the dead (e.g., raise Jairus' daughter from the dead in Mark 5 and raise Lazarus from the dead in John 11) and control nature (e.g., Jesus' walking on water in Matthew 14, Mark 6 & John 6). Praying to Jesus allows Christians to experience such miraculous powers today.
- The Bible also records the followers of Jesus having miraculous powers – e.g., Peter walked on water following Jesus (Matthew 14, Mark 6 & John 6). Peter healed the lame man at the temple (Acts 3). In Joppa, Peter raised Tabitha from the dead. (Acts 9)

- The Roman Catholic Church claims that followers of Jesus continue to have such miraculous powers. The 'Congregation of the Causes of Saints' investigates miraculous claims, validating which ones are genuine. For the Church to canonise someone as a saint, they need to have performed at least two miracles. For example, before being canonised as a saint, Mother Teresa (1910-97) performed two miracles of healing: curing a woman with a lump in her abdomen and a man who had brain abscesses.

- Charismatic evangelical churches also claim to have such miraculous powers. Rejecting 'cessationism' (the claim that the miracles in the Bible no longer happen today), these churches claim to have miraculous gifts of healing, prophecy and speaking in tongues (a blessed form of communication with God).

- Liberal Christians reject both Catholic and charismatic evangelical claims to have miraculous powers. They reject that miracles even occurred in the Bible. Rudolf Bultmann, for example, argued that a belief in miracles results from confusing the power of the Christian message (its 'proclamation' or 'kerygma') with causal powers (e.g., the power to cure physical illnesses). Clearly distinguishing between the persuasive power of the Christian message from the physical power of causation allows us to 'demythologise' the Bible – i.e.., recognise Christianity's proclamation (spiritual message) to be true, but its miraculous (physically causal) claims to be false.

ATONEMENT

- Jesus' crucifixion acts as the 'atonement' for sin, allowing us to be at-one with God following our alienation from God.

- For most Christians, following St Augustine's interpretation of the Bible, this alienation from God resulted from the Fall in Genesis 3 – Adam and Eve ate from the 'tree of the knowledge of good and evil' and this 'first sin' resulted in 'original sin' (the corruption of human nature). Alienated from God's goodness, we cannot save ourselves. Only God can save us through His 'grace'.

- God saves us (we do not save ourselves) by sending His Son to die on the cross for the 'redemption' for our sins – i.e., he pays the price for those sins. If we accept this gift of forgiveness, we can experience reconciliation with God through the atonement. If we refuse to accept this gift of forgiveness, we remain alienated from God and so lack 'eternal life' and experience 'damnation' (hell) rather than 'salvation' (heaven).

RESURRECTION

- By accepting Jesus' redemption of our sins on the cross, and so atonement with God, we come to share in the resurrection – the conquering of sin and death by sharing in the life of God revealed in Christ.

- The 'particular resurrection' of Jesus' rising from the dead is seen to be the 'first fruits' of everyone rising from the dead at the 'general resurrection'. (1 Corinthians 15) To experience this eternal life of God, we have to repent of our selfishness so that God's grace might work in our hearts.

- For conservative Christians, the resurrection involves factually rising from the dead. For liberal Christians, the resurrection involves seeing one's life to belong to God and not oneself. In belonging to God, we share in eternal life.

Recall the definitions ... quiz yourself both ways!

Key word	Definition
Old Testament	First main section of the Bible, seen to prefigure the New Testament
Covenants	Formal agreements between God and humans
Covenant list	Noahic, Abrahamic, Mosaic, Davidic and New Covenant
New Covenant	Christians share in the life of God by sharing in the body and blood of Christ, celebrated in communion.
Incarnation	Jesus is the eternal Son or word of God made flesh
Christ's nature	Jesus is fully human and fully God, allowing us to know God in Christ
Virgin birth	Jesus' mother is the human Mary and his Father is God.
First sin	The sin that Adam and Eve committed in the Garden of Eden (Genesis 3)
Original sin	The corruption of human nature that resulted from the first sin
Baptism	Jesus' cousin John the Baptist baptised with water in the river Jordan, demanding repentance
Holy Spirit	John claims that Jesus will go on to baptise with the Holy Spirit before baptises Jesus himself with water.
Trinity	God the Father is heard as a voice in Jesus' baptism; God the Son is incarnated as Jesus; God the Holy Spirit is present as a dove. These 'three persons' are claimed to be of one 'substance' or nature in the Nicene Creed of 325AD.
Temptations	Following the baptism, Jesus resists the devil's temptations of pleasure (bread), power (kingdoms) and vanity (throwing himself off a temple so as to be caught by angels).
Miracles	*Dunamis* or power in Greek, and include supernatural acts of healing, exorcism, controlling nature and resurrection. Conservative Christians see miracles to be both literally true according to the 'inerrancy' of scripture. Liberal Christians like Bultmann see miracles to be 'mythological' expressions of the Christian proclamation (*kerygma*).
David Hume	In *Enquiries Concerning Human Understanding*, Hume argues that there is more evidence for the consistency of the laws of nature than there is evidence for miraculous acts.
James Keller	In his *Moral Argument Against Miracles*, Keller argues that particular acts of divine intervention seem unfair on people not helped in this way.
Rudolf Bultmann	Miracles, like magic, are confused ideas characteristic of the Bible and indeed all ancient thought. To properly understand the Bible proclamation (*kerygma*), we need to extract it from those confused ideas of supernatural causation – i.e., demythologise the Bible teaching.
John Shelby Spong	Anglican Bishop who argues that the real function of miracles is not a demonstration of supernatural causation, but of making clear what it means to be truly human.
Healing blind man	In John 9, Jesus heals a blind man by spitting on earth to create mud to apply to the man's eyes. After washing in the pool of Siloam the man regains his sight.

212 Founders & Leaders

IGCSE 2 Religious Studies

Key word	Definition
Pharisees	Jews concerned with making obedience to the law central to the Jewish faith and condemn Jesus and the man who was blind.
Sabbath	Commanded day of rest (Exodus 20) on which Jesus was criticised by the Pharisees for healing people
Son of Man	Jesus' way of referring to himself
Blindness	Jesus identifies physical blindness with spiritual blindness, claiming that the Pharisees' focus on obedience is blind to the real life of God.
Albert Schweitzer	Wrote *Quest for the Historical Jesus* in which he argued that Jesus had an eschatological interpretation of scripture
Eschatological	Viewing history in terms of its bringing about an end-time or higher purpose.
Juridical	Viewing history in terms of obedience or disobedience to the law.
Niddah	Hebrew for menstruating woman, who is declared to be unclean according to the Old Testament book Leviticus. Those who touch such a person become unclean.
Woman with issue of blood	Woman with a permanent issue of blood touches Jesus' cloak, but instead of making Jesus unclean, she is cleaned and healed. (Mark 5)
Literal interpretation	Miracles are factually accurate, describing supernatural forces. This interpretation is characteristic of conservative Christians (e.g., Catholics and Baptists)
Symbolic interpretation	Miracles are theological proclamations ('kerygma') rather than factual descriptions helping us to better understand God. This is characteristic of liberal Christians (e.g., many in the Church of England and Anglican Church of America).
Sermon on the Mount	Matthew 5, summarising Jesus' teachings in terms of Beatitudes, Antitheses and the life of discipleship
1. Beatitudes	8 characteristics of blessedness (godliness) in 3 sections: a person's real needs (1–3), the search for God (4–6) and for God's purpose or 'kingdom' (8). The last 2 characteristics concern the disciples' needs.
2. Antitheses	6 sayings that challenge the Old Testament law in order to highlight the purpose of those laws – their fulfilment. Jesus challenges the law on murder, adultery, divorce, oaths, retribution and love of neighbour.
3. Life of discipleship	Reject outward show of religious observance (obedience) and simply live a godly life. The Lord's prayer is an example of such an honest and heartfelt relationship to God. In this way, people will have the 'treasures' of heaven and enter the 'narrow gateway', building their faith on secure foundations.
Pesach	Passover meal, which Jesus celebrated with his disciples before being arrested, sharing bread as his body and wine as his blood in this meal.
Judas Iscariot	Apostle who betrayed Jesus for 30 pieces of silver.
Garden of Gethsemane	Jesus prays here for the 'cup of suffering' to be taken from him, but he is arrested by Jewish soldiers, telling Peter not to fight.
Herod Antipas	Typically called King Herod, the Jewish leader who interrogated Jesus on his arrest before sending him to Pontius Pilate.
Pontius Pilate	Roman Governor who was forced by the Jewish crowds to execute Jesus for claiming to be the 'King of the Jews'.
Golgotha	'Place of a Skull', which is the place Jesus was executed.

IGCSE 2 Religious Studies

Key word	Definition
Abraham	Almost sacrifices his son Isaac as a demonstration of his commitment to God, but God does not require this. (Genesis 22)
Pesach	The Passover when the angel of death passes over the Jewish families as it kills the firstborn of the Egyptians. The sacrifice of the lamb and its blood on the doors of the Jews made this possible.
Redemption	Jesus' sacrifice pays the price of our sin, allowing us to be reconciled with God after 'original sin' had alienated us from God.
Atonement	A state of oneness with God made possible by Jesus' redemption for our sins in his crucifixion.
Joseph of Arimathea	Jewish leader who gave his family tomb to Jesus.
Resurrection	Literally someone's coming back from the dead and theologically the overcoming of sin and death to reveal the 'new creation'.
Spiritual body	St Paul's term for the resurrection body, which is claimed to be 'imperishable' and 'of heaven'. It is contrasted with the 'natural body'.
Particular resurrection	Jesus' conquers sin and death by rising from the tomb on the third day after his crucifixion to reveal 'eternal life' or the life of God.
'First fruits'	Jesus' resurrection is the 'first fruits' of the general resurrection (1 Corinthians 15)
General resurrection	Everybody's rising from the dead at the second coming of Jesus at the end time, either sharing in eternal life or being condemned to hell.
Parousia	Second coming of Jesus
N.T. Wright	Conservative Christian arguing for a literal interpretation of the resurrection.
Marcus Borg	Liberal Christian arguing for only a symbolic interpretation of the resurrection.
Incarnation	God's word or Son becoming flesh as Jesus (John 1)
Miraculous powers	Catholic 'Congregation of the Causes of Saints' validates contemporary miracles. Charismatic evangelical churches also believe in miracles.
Cessationism	Miracles no longer occur after Biblical times
Justification by faith	St. Paul's term in the letters (Epistles) to the Romans and to the Galatians claiming that salvation is through God's grace and not by our own efforts ('justification by works')

Test yourself

(a) Outline **two** of Jesus' teachings about discipleship. (4)

(b) Explain the significance of Jesus Christ's life for Christians today. (6)

(c) "Jesus' crucifixion is the most important event in the life of Jesus Christ."
Discuss this statement considering the arguments for and against.
   In your answer you should include:
   - reference to teachings
   - other (divergent) points of view – either within the religion or from other religions
   - your opinion/point of view using reasoned arguments
   - a balanced conclusion. (10)

2.1.2b Founders & Leaders: Martin Luther King

REVISED

GENERIC SYLLABUS REQUIREMENTS
The importance of historical or contemporary religious leaders.

CHRISTIAN SYLLABUS REQUIREMENTS
The importance and teaching of an important Christian leader, other than the founder.

Martin Luther King

REVISED

> **Key point**
>
> Martin Luther King (1929-1968) was a Baptist Minister and civil rights activist who challenged racial discrimination in America through passive resistance.

- Martin Luther King had resented whites due to the "racial humiliation" he endured: segregation is the enforced separation of different racial groups in a country, community, or establishment.
- At the age of 18, he joined the Church due to "an inner urge to serve humanity." King became a Minister in the Baptist Church – an evangelical denomination of Christianity, which emphasises preaching and witnessing to the 'good news' of Christ.
- King's ministry was focused on people's rights and he advocated 'nonviolence' and 'civil disobedience' as part of a programme of 'passive resistance' against injustice. For example, he would recommend that people disobey unjust laws but not fight back when arrested. He also recommended that people boycott businesses guilty of racial segregation.
- His programme of passive resistance was influenced by Tolstoy's *The Kingdom of God is Within You*, which forcefully presented Jesus' non-violent resistance to Jewish and Roman power. King was also influenced by the political protests of Ghandi against the British Empire (who had also been influenced by Tolstoy's book).
- King's struggle against injustice began early in his ministry when in 1955, Rosa Parks was arrested for refusing to give up her seat on a city bus to a white passenger as required by some Southern State's segregation laws ('Jim Crow laws').
- King helped to organise a boycott of the bus company that lasted for 385 days. King was arrested, jailed and his house was bombed, attracting significant media attention.
- The boycott was successful and the United States District Court issued a ruling in 1956 in Browder v Gayle that racial segregation must be ended.
- King helped found the Southern Christian Leadership Conference (SCLC), which coordinated passive resistance to segregation amongst the churches.
- In 1963, the SCLC campaigned against racial segregation and economic injustice in Birmingham, Alabama. They adopted non-violent but confrontational tactics so as to attract media attention.

- King's strategy was to provoke mass arrests provoked by the SCLC's breaking what they saw to be unjust laws. In that way, King intended to "create a situation so crisis-packed that it will inevitably open the door to negotiation."

> **Mistake to avoid**
>
> Do not confuse Martin Luther King (the 20th century civil rights activist) with Martin Luther (the 16th century German Protestant Reformer).

- Early in to the campaign, King was arrested and jailed. This was his 13th arrest out of 29. In his cell, he composed his "Letter from Birmingham Jail", which has gone on to be famous. In this letter, he defends the strategy of non-violent civil disobedience, arguing: "We know through painful experience that freedom is never voluntarily given by the oppressor; it must be demanded by the oppressed." He notes how the American Revolution broke British law and how Hitler used the law to oppress people.

- The Birmingham Police Department, under Eugene "Bull" Connor, employed water cannon and police dogs against the protesters, including children. The media presented the police's violence against mostly peaceful protestors, attracting significant sympathy for the protestors.

- Connor lost his job, restrictions on blacks were lifted and King's reputation was enhanced.

- In 1963, King helped to organise a march into Washington to demand civil rights legislation.

- In this march, Martin Luther King delivered his speech 'I have a dream'. It was inspirational, fusing the Christian vision of the kingdom of God in which all people are respected, with the American Declaration of Independence, which states: 'We hold these truths to be self-evident, that all men are created equal, that they are endowed by their Creator with certain unalienable Rights, that among these are Life, Liberty and the pursuit of Happiness.' Celebrating the ideal of freedom from oppression, King presents a powerful vision of people living together in harmony: "I have a dream that my four little children will one day live in a nation where they will not be judged by the colour of their skin, but by the content of their character."

- The SCLC under King's direction helped to bring about the Civil Rights Act of 1964 and the Voting Rights Act of 1965, resulting in desegregation and black rights to vote and work.

- In 1965, King was stabbed by a mentally ill black woman while he was signing copies of his book *Strive Towards Freedom*. King received emergency surgery but survived.

- King went on to oppose American involvement in the Vietnam War.

- In 1968, King and the SCLC organized the 'Poor People's Campaign': 'a multiracial army of the poor' to achieve an 'economic bill of rights' for poor Americans.

- In this campaign, King delivered his 'I've Been to the Mountaintop' speech in which he discusses death threats against him. 'Like anybody, I would like to live a long life. Longevity has its place. But I'm not concerned about that now. I just want to do God's will. And He's allowed me to go up to the mountain. And I've looked over. And I've seen the promised land. I may not get there with you. But I want you to know tonight, that we, as a people, will get to the promised land.'

- The next day, at the age of 39, King was assassinated. James Earl Ray, a white man who already had a criminal record for mail fraud, burglary and armed robbery – was charged with King's murder.

- The assassination led to a nationwide wave of race riots, although many leaders called people back to King's ideal of nonviolence.
- There were conspiracy theories about King's death. The U.S. Department of Justice investigated these and in 2000 reported finding no evidence supporting the allegations. Some of the conspiracy theorists were also discovered to be making up allegations for financial gain.

Malcolm X

REVISED

> **Key point**
>
> Malcolm X is not a "significant Christian"; he is a Muslim. He is only included here to help you evaluate Martin Luther King's position in a 10-mark question. Malcolm X rejected both King's non-violent resistance and his ideal of social integration.

- Malcolm Little (1925–1965) spent most of his adolescence in foster homes and in 1946 was arrested for burglary.
- While serving 10 years in prison, he joined the Nation of Islam.
- The "Nation of Islam" fused many traditional Islamic beliefs about community cohesion and discipline with its own ideas of black supremacy and black separatism.
- The Nation of Islam required followers to give up their previous surnames and adopt the letter X before adopting a new Arabic name. Otherwise, they could retain the letter X to show that their surname was taken from them by slavery. This is what Malcolm X did.
- Malcolm X mocked Martin Luther King, calling him a 'chump'. He called the 1963 March on Washington, in which King gave his "I have a dream" speech, as 'the farce on Washington'.
- Against King's non-violent resistance, Malcom X argued for resistance "by any means necessary".
- Against King's ideal of social integration, Malcom X argued in favour of African Americans separating from whites into their own country.
- After claiming that President Kennedy's assassination was in some sense deserved, a "case of chickens coming home to roost," the Nation of Islam expelled Malcolm X as a leader. Malcolm X rejected the Nation of Islam in favour of more mainstream Sunni Islam.
- The Nation of Islam's leader Louis Farrakhan condemned Malcolm X's "betrayal", arguing that "hypocrites like Malcolm should have their heads cut off". Armed with a semi-automatic rifle, Malcom X tried to defend himself, but Nation of Islam members killed him in 1965, shooting him with a sawed-off shotgun and semi-automatic handguns.

IGCSE 2 Religious Studies

Recall the definitions ... quiz yourself both ways!

TESTED ☐

Key word	Definition
Passive resistance	A strategy of 'nonviolence' and 'civil disobedience' (e.g., breaking laws) so as to highlight the injustice of the oppressors
Sermon on the Mount	In Matthew 5, the Beatitudes, Jesus sees the 'peacemakers' to be blessed. Inhis Antitheses, he rejects the retribution of 'eye for an eye' (Exodus 21) in favour of 'turning the other cheek' when attacked.
Leo Tolstoy	*The Kingdom of God is Within You*, advocating nonviolent resistance
Ghandi	Advocated nonviolent resistance against the British Empire
Rosa Parks	In 1955, she was arrested for refusing to give up her seat on a city bus to a white passenger; King helped to successfully boycott the bus company for 385 days.
SCLC	Southern Christian Leadership Conference is the group of churches that King represented.
29	The number of times Martin Luther King was arrested
Letter from Birmingham Jail	Famous letter of 1963 defending his strategy of political activism through non-violent civil disobedience.
Eugene "Bull" Connor	Head of Police in Birmingham, Alabama who used water cannon and dogs on the protestors.
Washington DC	March of civil rights activists into Washington DC in 1963 and King's famous 'I have a dream' speech
Civil Rights Act	Act in 1964 ending discrimination on the on the basis of race, color, religion, sex or national origin.
Voting Rights Act	Act in 1965 ending racial discrimination in voting rights
Poor People's Campaign	In 1968, the SCLC, represented by King, aimed to achieve an 'economic bill of rights' for poor Americans
I've Been to the Mountaintop	Speech of 1968 in favour of the rights of Memphis sanitary public works employees in which King refers to death threats
James Earl Ray	White man charged with King's assassination
Malcolm X	Malcom Little's name after joining the Nation of Islam in prison.
Against passive resistance	"Resistance by any means necessary" was Malcom X's phrase for rejecting passive resistance
Nation of Islam	A religious movement that believed in black supremacy.
Louis Farrakhan	Leader of Nation of Islam who called for Malcom X's death when he left that religious group

212b Founders & Leaders

44   IGCSE 2 Religious Studies

> **Test yourself**
>
> (a) Outline **two** contributions to Christianity of one significant Christian other than Jesus, either historical or contemporary. (4)
>
> (b) Explain the teaching of of one significant Christian other than Jesus, either historical or contemporary. (6)
>
> (c) "'The Bible is the only teaching a Christian needs."
> Discuss this statement considering the arguments for and against.
>   In your answer you should include:
>   - reference to teachings
>   - other (divergent) points of view – either within the religion or from other religions
>   - your opinion/point of view using reasoned arguments
>   - a balanced conclusion. (10)

2.2 Celebrations & Pilgrimage

Topic 2.2.1a Festivals & Celebration: Christmas

REVISED ☐

GENERIC SYLLABUS REQUIREMENTS
The principal festivals of the religion, including their history and importance. How the festivals are 'observed', including their traditions and rituals.

CHRISTIAN SYLLABUS REQUIREMENTS.
Christmas' importance and how it is celebrated.

Christian calendar & its main festivals

REVISED ☐

> **Key point**
>
> The Christian Calendar begins with Advent (preparation for Christmas), includes two major festivals (Christmas itself and Easter), "ordinary time" and lesser festivals (e.g., Pentecost).

- The Christian calendar is structured around two major celebrations: Christmas, marking the incarnation of God (God's becoming flesh in Christ) and Easter marking the resurrection (the victory over sin and death (first realised by Jesus rising from the dead). Before each celebration, there is a 'penitential' season for believers to spiritually prepare: Advent precedes Christmas and Lent precedes Easter. The rest of the Christian calendar is termed the 'ordinary' season.
- The celebratory seasons of Christmas and Easter are typically celebrated in the 'liturgical colours' of white or gold. The penitential seasons are typically celebrated in purple. The ordinary season is typically celebrated in green.
- There are also Feast Days for special events – e.g., Pentecost, which celebrates the descent of the Holy Spirit upon the apostles on the 50th day after Easter Sunday and has the liturgical colour red). Epiphany, which traditionally occurs on January 6th or on the first Sunday after January 1st, celebrates the wise men visiting the Christ child, which has the liturgical colour white. Saints days typically celebrate Christian martyrs in the liturgical colour red.
- The Roman Catholic, Eastern Orthodox and Anglican churches use the Christian calendar to structure their worship. Some of the more

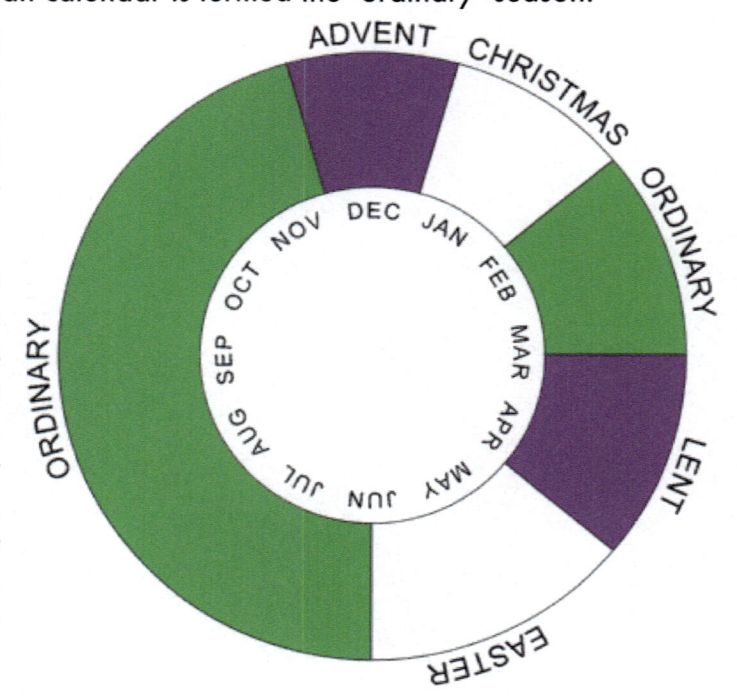

46   IGCSE 2 Religious Studies

evangelical Christians (e.g., many Baptists) follow Martin Luther's (1483-1546) *'sola scriptura'* principle, which sees the Bible to be the only thing necessary for salvation. They therefor reject the Christian calendar as a human invention that distracts us from living out the Gospel message every day of our lives.

History of the Christmas celebration   REVISED

> **Key point**
>
> Given that there is no Biblical record of the date of Christ's birth, Christmas is celebrated on the day of the solstice and was fixed on the date 25 December when the Gregorian calendar was introduced in the 16th century AD.

- Christmas celebrates the birth of Jesus, although there is no Biblical or historical record about the precise date when this occurred. The Christian Church chose the winter solstice as the date for Jesus' birth since this is the shortest day of the year; following Jesus' birth therefore, the light comes into the world, shown by the days becoming longer.
- The day of the solstice was also closely related to the celebration of the god Mithras, who was the god of the sun. Some say that placing Christ's birth on that date allowed Christmas to enjoy the same associations of this 'Roman mystery cult' worshipping the power of life.
- In October 1582, Pope Gregory XIII updated the Western calendar in the light of developments in modern science. This 'improved calendar' was eventually accepted by all nations. Christmas was fixed according to this calendar on the 25th December. Easter, by contrast, continued to be calculated according to the earlier 'lunar' calendar, which calculates dates based upon observing the moon.)
- The Eastern Orthodox Church however, rejects using the 'Gregorian calendar' to calculate the date of Christmas and remain loyal to the lunar calendar. The date they celebrate Christmas therefore changes similar to the date of Easter. Currently, Christmas is celebrated in early January in Eastern Orthodox countries.
- In 17th century England, some of the 'Puritan' Christians, keen to return to an authentically Biblical faith and to reject Roman Catholic traditions, rejected celebrating Christmas. They considered this celebratory festival to involve the 'trappings of popery' and instead insisted upon a dutiful and sober faith.
- In the UK, Christmas became a bank holiday in 1834. Boxing Day, the day after Christmas, was also made a bank holiday in 1871. The image of Christmas as a day of relaxation from work and of being generous to one's neighbour was reinforced by Charles Dickens' novel *A Christmas Carol*.
- The Christmas tree was first introduced in Germany under the Lutheran Church (members of the church of Martin Luther who broke with Catholicism in 1517. The tree is decorated typically with a star on top to celebrate the nativity star that led the three wise men to worship Jesus.
  - Father Christmas derives from stories about St Nicholas, a 4th-century Greek bishop from Myra, now in modern-day Turkey. In one tale, he met a poor man who was on the brink of selling his own daughters into slavery. Under the cover of darkness, the

saint anonymously threw three bags of gold down the chimney to provide dowries for the girls (i.e., money necessary for their being married). The gold landed in their stockings, which were drying by the fire.

Christmas' importance: Messiah's birth

> **Key point**
>
> Christmas marks the fulfilment of the Jewish Messianic tradition – of a promised leader who will guide God's people along His path.

- The birth of Christ, celebrated at Christmas, is claimed to fulfil Old Testament prophecy.
- In Genesis 2, God creates 'Adam' who falls from a right relationship to God. (Genesis 3) A number of 'covenants' or formal agreements between God and humanity are established to restore a right relationship between God and humanity, but each one is betrayed. The birth of Christ marks the 'new Adam' (Hebrews 2) who will fulfil the 'covenants'.
- Even the Mosaic law (the 613 rules of traditional Judaism with the 10 commandments at their heart) are used by humans to claim that they are 'purer' than others instead of for their right purpose – to fulfil God's kingdom on earth as it is in heaven (e.g., the aim of the Lord's Prayer of Matthew 6 & Luke 11).
- To lead God's people towards a right relationship to God, a Messiah (Hebrew for 'anointed leader' and 'Christ' in Greek) is promised.
- The Book of Isaiah prophesies the Messiah: 'Therefore the Lord himself shall give you a sign; Behold, the young woman [virgin] shall conceive, and bear a son and shall call his name Immanuel.' (Isaiah 7) [Immanuel is Hebrew for 'God is with us'.]
- Isaiah 9 also refers to the promised Messiah as follows: 'For a child has been born to us, a son given to us and the authority is upon his shoulder and the wondrous adviser, the mighty God, the everlasting Father, called his name "the prince of peace."'
- Isaiah 53 refers to how the promised Messiah will suffer for our salvation: 'He was hurt for our wrong-doing. He was crushed for our sins. He was punished so we would have peace. He was beaten so we would be healed.'
- The promised Messiah will come from the line of the Jewish king David as prophesied by the Old Testament book Ezekiel 37.
- Matthew's Gospel claims that Jesus is the fulfilment of the prophecy of the Messiah/Christ. It begins by noting in Matthew 1 that Jesus is the 'son of David' born of a 'virgin', fulfilling the prophecy of Isaiah 7.

- Jesus' life echoes the life of the people of Israel: e.g., just as the Jews were in the desert for 40 years after their escape from Egypt (Exodus) so Jesus was in the wilderness being tempted by the devil for 40 days (Matthew 4). Just as the Torah (law) involves 5 books (Genesis, Exodus, Leviticus, Numbers & Deuteronomy) so Jesus presents 5 major discourses in Matthew's Gospel: the sermon on the Mount (ch. 5-7); Mission Discourse (ch. 10); Parables of the Kingdom (ch. 13); Church life & discipline (ch. 18) and Discourse on the end times (ch. 23-25).

- Simeon was a devout Jew awaiting the Messiah, and on seeing Jesus he recognised him as the Messiah, claiming that his 'eyes have seen Your (God's) salvation'. (Luke 2)

- St Augustine argued that the prophecy of the Messiah/Christ was necessary for preparing our minds for recognising God's character in Jesus: 'It was necessary that all this should be prophesied, announced in advance. We needed to be told so that our minds might be prepared.' (Exposition of Psalm 109)

- Christmas is therefore firstly important in fulfilling the prophecy of the Messiah, since it marks the birth of the promised leader who will restore us to a right relationship to God.

Christmas' importance: incarnation

> **Key point**
>
> Christmas marks the birth of Jesus, understood as the "word" or "Son of God" (one "person" of the Trinity) becoming flesh in Jesus.

- The synoptic Gospels of Matthew, Mark & Luke all present Jesus' temptation by the devil God is Trinitarian for Christianity – Father, Son and Holy Spirit (Nicene Creed of 325AD). The 'Son' is the eternal 'word' or 'logos' of God that becomes flesh in Jesus: 'And the word became flesh.' (John 1) Christmas celebrates the incarnation – God's becoming flesh in Christ.

- Christmas celebrates God's incarnation, in which the character of a human reveals the character of God. As such, Jesus is claimed to be 'fully man and fully God' in traditional Christology (the study of Christ's nature).

- This union of God and human is marked in the Christian story by the 'virgin birth' (Matthew 1 & Luke 1) – Jesus has the human Mary as his mother and God as his Father.

- The angel Gabriel announces to Mary (in the Annunciation) that she will give birth to the 'Son of the Most High' through the 'power of the Holy Spirit'. (Luke 1)

- Through the Son of God, we come to know God more fully than appeals to laws or customs: *'Long ago, at many times and in many ways, God spoke to our fathers by the prophets, but in these last days he has spoken to us by his Son, whom he appointed the heir of all things, through whom also he created the world.'* (Hebrews 1)

Observance of Advent

> **Key point**
>
> Advent is a "penitential season" leading up to Christmas in which Christians spiritually prepare (perhaps through Bible reading or fasting) for celebrating Christmas.

- Advent is not Christmas but how Christians prepare for Christmas.
- Advent begins on the 4th Sunday before Christmas. It marks the beginning of the Christian calendar – i.e., the Christian calendar does not start on 1 January, but 4 weeks before Christmas.
- Advent means in Latin 'coming towards' and it is a time of preparation and anticipation for meeting God in the Christ child.
- Advent has also traditionally been a time of penitence (recollecting one's sins) and fasting (disciplining oneself) so that one is ready to meet God in Christ. It typically involves the liturgical colour purple, characteristic of penitential seasons.
- More traditional churches (e.g., Catholic, Eastern Orthodox and Anglican) use an Advent wreath to structure the 4 weeks of Advent before Christmas. Other churches (e.g., many Baptist churches) might reject such traditions, appealing to Martin Luther's *sola scriptura* principle (the Bible alone is necessary for salvation).
- Each candle represents important events in the revelation of God's word before the word's incarnation as Christ. Each week involves readings in the lectionary (set readings of the church)
    1. Week 1: Patriarchs (Church Fathers such as Abraham) [the candle is purple]
    2. Week 2: Prophets (Isaiah)) [the candle is purple]
    3. Week 3: John the Baptist) [the candle is pink]
    4. Week 4: Mary the mother of Jesus [the candle is purple]
    5. Christmas Day: Jesus Christ [the candle is white and is placed at the centre of the other 4 candles]
- The season of Advent awaits the celebration of the incarnation of God in Christ in Bethlehem at Christmas, but it also looks forward to the end time ('*eschaton*' in Greek): the time when Jesus returns at his 'second coming' ('*parousia*' in Greek) to judge the world and bring about the 'new creation' (2 Corinthians 5) – God's kingdom on earth as it is in heaven.

Observance of Christmas

REVISED ☐

> **Key point**
>
> Established practices for celebrating Christmas.

- On Christmas Eve, there is often a service of Nine Lessons and Carols to celebrate God's becoming flesh at Christmas. The 'lessons' or Bible readings tell of the fall of humanity, the promise of the Messiah or Christ and finally the birth of Christ. The 9th lesson is the first chapter of the Gospel of John, which is introduced as follows: 'St John unfolds the great mystery of the Incarnation.' Each of the lessons are interspersed with Christmas carols. The Reverend Benson devised the first Nine Lessons and Carols service in 1880 in Cornwall's Truro Cathedral. It was taken up and made famous by King's College, Cambridge.

- Christmas typically is celebrated with a Nativity Scene, in which statues of the holy family (Mary, Joseph with Jesus in a 'manger' or feeding trough) are placed alongside the shepherds and the animals in a stable under a star. This is to remember Jesus' birth, when Mary and Joseph found no inn to stay in when they had to go to Bethlehem to be registered for a Roman census. The star directed the shepherds to worship the Christian child in Luke's Gospel and the three wise men of the East (Magi or 'kings') in Matthew's Gospel. Sometimes, statues of the three wise men are also included in the Nativity Scene, although traditionally these were added on January 6 in the Epiphany. St Francis of Assisi is claimed to have created the first nativity scene in 1223 to help people more clearly experience the Bible story.

- Catholic and Anglican Churches typically have a midnight mass, which is a communion service in which believers share in the body and blood of Christ. In this way, Christmas celebrates believers becoming 'adopted' children of God (Ephesians 1) since they share in the character of God revealed in Christ. In this way, Catholics celebrate Christmas the moment it turns midnight to show their eager expectation of this day.

- Christians typically give presents at Christmas to celebrate God's gift of his Son, the eternal word's incarnation in Jesus. (John 1) Christmas has become heavily commercialised however, meaning that the gifts are now often seen as more important than the experience of God through Christ. Many Christians are therefore cautious about giving too much importance to presents in case it encourages self-centredness rather than sharing in Christ's life of love and of service.

- Christians also typically send Christmas cards as a token of their love for their family members and for their friends. These cards decorate the house, contributing to the joy of Christmas day.

- On Christmas day, Christians typically celebrate Christmas with a communion service in the morning. The wider family (grandparents, etc.) typically gather together to celebrate the love that has kept the family together through time and after the church service there is a celebratory meal.

Christmas ends on the Epiphany

> **Key point**
>
> The season of Christmas (Christmastide) last 12 days & ends on the Epiphany.

- Christmas traditionally runs for 12 days, ending on the Epiphany on 6 January.
- The Epiphany on January 6th focuses on how God's revelation in Christ is first revealed to the Gentiles (non-Jews) as the three wise men were not Jewish, but from the East. This prefigures Christianity being a universal religion – a faith for all peoples rather than one specific to the Semites (the Jewish people). The three wise men give the Christ child gold, to represent his being a king, frankincense to represent his being holy and myrrh (an embalming oil) to represent his dying for our sins.
- Traditionally, the wise men were added to the Nativity Scene on Epiphany although sometimes they are added on Christmas day.

Recall the definitions ... quiz yourself both ways

Key word	Definition
Christian calendar	Christian year, starting with Advent and moving through the two principal feasts of Christmas and Easter ending with Ordinary Time.
Liturgical worship	Worship that is formal and structured around the Christian calendar, characteristic of Roman Catholic Church, Eastern Orthodox Church and Church of England.
Non-liturgical worship	Worship that is informal and typically is not structured around the Christian calendar. 17th century AD 'Puritan' Christians and Quakers reject the Christian calendar.
17th century AD Puritans	Rejected traditions such as Christmas and Easter based upon the Bible so as to focus simply on the teachings of the Bible.
Quakers	Religious Society of Friends who rejected religious traditions in favour of focusing on the *agapeic* love they claimed was central to the Bible's teaching.

Key word	Definition
	HISTORY OF CHRISTMAS
Winter solstice	Shortest day of the year, which has come to be identified with the birth of Christ (Christmas)
Mithras	Roman god of light, whose festival was on a similar date to Christmas.
Pope Gregory XIII	Updated the Western calendar on October 1582 to the solar calendar. This 'improved calendar' was eventually accepted by all nations. Christmas was fixed according to this calendar on the 25th December.
Eastern Orthodox Church	Rejected using the 'Gregorian calendar', remaining loyal to the old lunar calendar meaning that Christmas changes date dependent upon full moons for this denomination.
1834	Christmas Day was made a Bank Holiday in the UK
1871	Boxing Day (the day after Christmas) was made a bank holiday in the UK.
St Nicholas	A 4th-century Greek bishop from Myra, now in modern-day Turkey, who saved a man from selling his daughters into slavery by putting money down through his chimney, landing in the daughters' stockings.
Hebrews 2	Jesus is the 'new Adam' who overcomes original sin that arose with the 'first sin' of Adam in the Garden of Eden (Genesis 3)
Isaiah 7	Prophecies that the Messiah will be born of a virgin/maiden.
Simeon	A devout man who claims his 'eyes have seen Your (God's) salvation' on seeing the Christ child. (Luke 2)
John 1	'The word became flesh' in the incarnation.
Hebrews 1	God now speaks to us in his Son in the incarnation.
Council of Nicaea	Church Council of 325AD declaring that God is Father, Son and Holy Spirit, and incarnated in Jesus.
Penitential Seasons	Times of fasting and self-discipline so as to be ready for experiencing God in the festivals of Christmas and of Easter.
	ADVENT
Advent	40-day Penitential Season for preparing to encounter God in Christ at Christmas.
Advent wreath	Candles in decorative ring of leaves to remember the key events that led up to the incarnation at Christmas.
Week 1	1st week of Advent remembers the Patriarchs of Church Fathers like Abraham. (purple candle)
Week 2	2nd week of Advent remembers the Prophets like Isaiah who prophesied the coming of the Messiah. (purple candle)
Week 3	3rd week of Advent remembers John the Baptist, who emphasised not obedience to the law, but the transformation of one's character, symbolised by baptism (ritual washing). (pink candle)
Week 4	4th week of Advent remembers the 'Virgin Mary' whose selfless love for her child made the life of *agapeic* love revealed in Christ possible. (purple candle)

TESTED

Key word	Definition
	CHRISTMASTIDE
Christmas Day	White candle in the centre of the wreath remembers the birth of Jesus as the Son of God, revealing God's life on earth as it is in heaven.
9 Lessons & Carols	A service of lessons and carols celebrating the lead-up to the birth of Christ. The final 'lesson' is the account of the incarnation in John 1.
Reverend Benson	Devised the first Nine Lessons and Carols service in 1880 in Cornwall's Truro Cathedral before it was made famous by King's College, Cambridge.
Midnight mass	A communion service in Catholic, Eastern Orthodox and Anglican churches to celebrate Christmas day at midnight.
Christmas gifts	To celebrate the gift of God's life revealed in Christ at Christmas
Christmas cards	Ways to express God's love to celebrate God's revealing His love for the world in giving to us His Son.
Family time	Christmas is a time to celebrate the love that a family shares in.
Nativity Scene	Models representing the birth of Jesus in a stable.
Epiphany	This celebrates the 3 wise men worshipping the Christ child 12 days after Christmas day on 6 January.

TESTED

Test yourself

(a) Outline **two** rituals associated with Christmas. (4)
(b) Explain the history of the celebration of Christmas. (6)
(c) "Christmas should be an exclusively Christian festival." Discuss.
Discuss this statement considering the arguments for and against.
  In your answer you should include:
  - reference to teachings
  - other (divergent) points of view – either within the religion or from other religions
  - your opinion/point of view using reasoned arguments
  - a balanced conclusion. (10)

2.2.1b Festivals & Celebration: Easter

CHRISTIAN SYLLABUS REQUIREMENTS.
The importance of Easter and how it is celebrated.

History of the Easter Festival

> **Key point**
>
> The celebration of Jesus' rising from the dead, understood as the 'particular resurrection' looking forward to the 'general resurrection' of conquering sin and death at the 'end time' ('*eschaton*'). This is prepared for in Lent and is celebrated from Easter Sunday through Ascension Day to Pentecost.

- Easter celebrates the particular resurrection (Jesus' conquering sin and death by rising from the dead) and looks forward to the general resurrection (in which all will be raised from the dead at the 'eschaton' [end time] at the '*parousia*' [second coming] of Christ.
- The Bishop Melito of Sardis records that the Easter festival was well established by the 2nd century AD.
- The Greek Christian Church history, Socrates Scholasticus (5th century AD) claims that Jesus did not require that Christians celebrate Easter (or Christmas), but that it arose universally in all churches from custom to commemorate the major events in Jesus' life.
- The 40-day season of Lent (a time of spiritual preparation, characterised by self-discipline) precedes the season of Easter. Lent remembers Jesus' 40 days in the desert being tempted, which occurred straight after his baptism. Saint Athanasius records that Lent was observed throughout the "whole world" by 339AD.
- The season of Easter (Eastertide) was agreed to last for 50 days, running from Easter Sunday to Pentecost (when the Holy Spirit descended upon the apostles as recorded in Acts 2). Another significant event in Eastertide was the Ascension of Jesus on the 40th day, in which the resurrected Christ bodily ascended to heaven.
- Easter was celebrated on various dates in the early church. The First Council of Nicaea (325AD) gave no specific rules about how Easter should be celebrated, but claimed that Easter's date should be distinct from festivals in the Jewish calendar and it should be agreed by all Christians.
- The date of Easter was calculated in relation to the Jewish Passover since the events follow Jesus' last supper, which was a celebration of *Pesach* or Passover. This celebrates the angel of death passing over the Jewish houses due to their having the blood of a lamb on their 'lintels' (door posts) but killing the first born of the Egyptians. This allowed the Jews to be freed from slavery.
- Unlike Christmas then, for which there is no Biblical evidence of its date, Easter is dated in relation to the Jewish dating of Passover, which is calculated according to the lunisolar calendar. Easter falls on the first full Moon after the spring equinox and is therefore known in the Christian calendar as the Paschal Full Moon.

IGCSE 2 Religious Studies

- The Puritan Churches of the 16th and 17th centuries, rejected the traditions of Easter celebrations, insisting upon a purely Biblically based faith. The Quakers (Religious Society of Friends) similarly rejected celebrating Easter, claiming that "every day is the Lord's day".
- Since Easter Sunday is not a working day, it has not needed to be made a bank holiday in Christian influenced cultures. In the UK, Good Friday (the day of crucifixion) and Easter Monday (the day after Easter Sunday) are bank holidays.

Easter's importance: fulfilling season of Lent

> **Key point**
>
> Lent remembers key events in the lead-up to Jesus's resurrection, celebrated at Easter.

- Lent is a season of spiritual discipline of 40 days as Christians prepare to experience the resurrection on Easter Sunday. Such preparatory seasons of self-discipline are called 'penitential' and are traditionally celebrated with the colour purple.
- Lent remembers Jesus' temptation in the desert following his baptism. As Luke records it: 'Jesus, full of the Holy Spirit, left the Jordan and was led by the Spirit into the wilderness, where for forty days he was tempted by the devil. He ate nothing during those days, and at the end of them he was hungry.' (Luke 4:1-2)
- ASH WEDNESDAY: Lent begins with Ash Wednesday in which Christians come before the priest to be 'ashed'. The priest makes the sign of the cross on the forehead of the Christian, with ash made from burning palm leaves from last year's Palm Sunday celebration (see below) mixed with a little oil. The priest says: 'Remember that you are dust and to dust you will return; turn away from sin and be faithful to Christ.' This encourages the Christian to be modest and to put all their trust in God.
'So I turned to the Lord God and pleaded with Him in prayer and petition, in fasting, and in sackcloth and ashes.' (Daniel 9)
- HOLY WEEK: This is the last week of Lent prior to Easter. This week focuses on Jesus' coming into Jerusalem, the capital of Israel, to challenge Judaism's traditional focus on obedience to the law in favour of his new focus on seeing God's purposes for oneself and sharing in the life of God.
- PALM SUNDAY: This is the first Sunday of Holy Week and involves Jesus riding into Jerusalem on a donkey, as prophesied. The crowds placed palm leaves before Jesus as a type of royal carpet for the Messiah to ride in on. Christians celebrate this with a procession in church, in which they hold up a palm leaf shaped in a cross. They often keep the palm-leaf cross throughout the year to remember Easter and Jesus' sacrifice and resurrection.
- MAUNDY THURSDAY: This is the Thursday of Holy Week in which Jesus celebrates *Pesach* (Passover) with his apostles in the synoptic Gospels (Matthew, Mark & Luke). Jesus celebrates this in a distinctive way, sharing his body (in the bread) and blood (in the wine). This becomes the basis of the 'eucharist' or 'communion', in which Christians share in the life of God through Christ. In John's Gospel, Maundy Thursday is when Jesus washes the feet of his disciples, indicating that he is the servant leader, concerned to satisfy the needs of those he serves. Christians mark this with the priest washing the feet of the congregation.

- GOOD FRIDAY: Following the celebration of *Pesach*, Jesus goes to the Garden of Gethsemane to pray and is arrested and eventually taken to Pontius Pilate, the Roman Governor, to be tried. Pilate tries to free him, but the Jewish crowds inspired by the Jewish leaders, demand that Jesus and not Barabbas is crucified. Jesus is flogged and crucified. Christians remember this by stripping religious decorations or covering it with purple sheets. The main service on Good Friday takes place between midday and 3 pm – Jesus is believed to have died at 3pm. In many churches, the service takes the form of a meditation based on the seven sayings or "last word", of Jesus on the cross, accompanied by hymns, prayers, and short sermons. The congregation leave in silence to mark the death of God's life on earth in Jesus.

- This service marks the atonement – Jesus dying for our sins so that forgiveness might be possible.

Easter Sunday in Eastertide

> **Key point**
>
> Easter Sunday is the main event in the season of Easter (Eastertide), celebrating Jesus' conquering sin and death by rising from the dead.

- Easter Sunday is the climax of Holy Week and more broadly Lent. Having challenged traditional Judaism's focus on the law on Palm Sunday and instituted the importance of sharing in the life of God on Maundy Thursday and revealed the life of self-sacrifice on Good Friday, Easter Sunday celebrates the transformed life that this makes possible – the resurrection.

- After Jesus had been taken down from the cross, Jesus is laid in the tomb of Joseph of Arimathea, wrapped in linen cloth with a large stone protecting the entrance. Mary Magdalene finds the stone rolled away and the body gone, only the linen cloth remaining. She asks what she thinks is the gardener where Jesus is, and finally recognises him as the resurrected Christ.

- Easter Sunday celebrates Jesus rising from the dead to conquer sin and death. It ends the fasting and self-discipline of Lent and celebrates the birth of new life, marked by Easter eggs and Easter bunnies.

- In Church, Easter begins with an Easter Vigil at dusk. A bonfire is lit with prayers and the Paschal (Easter) candle is lit. This is a large, decorated candle and baptismal candles, etc. are lit from the light of this main candle, representing Christ as the light of the world.

- Studs with incense inside are placed in the candle, representing the 5 wounds of Christ in the shape of a cross (top stud for crown of thorns, bottom stud for nail in feet, 2 side studs for nails in hands, and the middle stud represents Jesus being speared in the side to ensure that he was dead before being brought down from the cross).

- The candle is typically decorated with the first and last letters of the alphabet (alpha and omega) to indicate that the God revealed in Christ is the beginning and end of all things (Revelation 22) – the source and purpose of our lives.
- The candle is taken into Church with a procession, with the priest chanting 'The light of Christ' and the congregation responding 'Thanks be to God'.
- Individual 'votive' candles are then lit from the Paschal candle, representing how Christians share in the life/light of God through Christ – they are 'adopted' children of God as they share in the life of the 'Son of God'.
- There are Bible readings and hymns celebrating Jesus' conquering sin and death, which first entered the world with the Fall in the Garden of Eden.

Ascension Day in Eastertide

REVISED

> **Key point**
>
> Celebrates Jesus' ascending to heaven 40 days after his resurrection.

- Ascension Day falls 40 days after Easter Sunday.
- Having conquered sin and death on Easter Sunday with Following his resurrection on Easter Sunday, Jesus appears to Mary Magdalene and then to his apostles. People typically fail to immediately recognise who Jesus is until he speaks with them or 'breaks bread' with them. Having conquered sin and death, Jesus bodily ascends to heaven in the Ascension, which is celebrated 40 days after Easter. The Feast of the Ascension is one of the ecumenically (i.e., universally) celebrated events in the Christian calendar.
- In Acts 1, Jesus promises that his followers will receive the Holy Spirit and Jesus is then 'taken up into a cloud while they were watching, and they could no longer see him.' There is a communion service with readings and hymns celebrating the Ascension.
- 17th century English Puritans and Quakers (Religious Society of Friends) do not celebrate such traditions created on the basis of scripture however, focusing instead on the Biblical or spiritual message.
- This is celebrated with white vestments (priestly clothing) and altar frontals (the material the covers the altar).

Pentecost in Eastertide

> **Key point**
>
> Celebrates the Holy Spirit coming upon the apostles 50 days after Jesus' resurrection.

- Pentecost falls 50 days after Easter Sunday and marks the end of Eastertide.
- Pentecost remembers the gift of the Holy Spirit. The Holy Spirit is the third 'person' of the Trinity of Father, Son and Holy Spirit - which is how Christians understand God.
- In Acts 2, the apostles are uncertain about how to witness to their faith following Jesus' ascension into heaven. In the 'upper room' in which they had experienced the 'last supper', they then experience the Holy Spirit resting upon them like 'tongues of fire'.
- By sharing in the Holy Spirit, the apostles are able to share in the life of God, shown by each one of them being able to understand each other when speaking in their own distinct language. (Acts 2)
- In 1 Corinthians 14, speaking in tongues is also described as an incomprehensible language to others since the person praying 'does not speak to men but to God'. (1 Corinthians 14)
- The Holy Spirit also allowed the apostles to perform miracles such as St Peter healing a lame beggar in Acts 3.
- The Feast of Pentecost is celebrated in the liturgical colour red to symbolise the fire of the Holy Spirit. The service includes Bible readings and hymns celebrating this experience, which has become fundamental to the authority of the church, since Catholic church leaders pass on the Holy Spirit through 'apostolic succession'.
- Less traditional churches would not have set Feast Days for Biblical events, focusing instead of the message of scripture.
- With the end of Pentecost, Eastertide ends.

Recall the definitions ... quiz yourself both ways

Key word	Definition
HISTORY OF EASTER	
Easter	Celebrates the particular resurrection of Jesus (his rising from the dead) and looks forward to the general resurrection at the end time (*eschaton*) at the second coming (*Parousia*) of Christ.
Bishop Melito	Bishop of Sardis who records that the Easter festival was well established by the 2nd century AD
Socrates Scholasticus	5th century AD church historian who claims that Jesus did not require that Christians celebrate Easter (or Christmas), but that it arose as a universal custom in the church.
Lent	Church prepares for Easter in penitential season of Lent, lasting 40 days. It is a time of spiritual preparation, characterised by self-discipline, remembering Jesus' 40 days in the desert being tempted.
Athanasius	Saint Athanasius records that Lent was observed throughout the "whole world" by 339AD
Council of Nicaea	The First Council of Nicaea (325AD) only claimed that Easter's date should be be agreed by all Christians
Paschal Full Moon	The date of Easter was calculated in relation to the Jewish Passover, falling on the first Sunday after the spring equinox.
Equinox	On the day of an equinox, daytime and nighttime are of approximately equal duration.
17th century Puritans	Rejected human traditions such as Easter in favour of focusing simply on the Biblical message.
Quakers	Religious Society of Friends who similarly rejected traditional festivals in favour of experiencing God's *agapeic* love.
Agape	Love of respect and appreciation, characteristic of Christian love.
Bank Holidays	Good Friday (day of crucifixion) and Easter Monday (day after Easter Sunday) are bank holidays in the UK.
LENT	
Lent	40-day penitential season of self-discipline remembering Christ's temptations in the desert for 40 days. It is a sombre season celebrated in purple.
Ash Wednesday	The first day of Lent in which people are traditionally ashed so as to remember that they are dust and to dust they will return.
Holy Week	The last week of Lent, which remembers Jesus' entrance into Jerusalem ending with his crucifixion.
Palm Sunday	The Sunday beginning Holy Week in which Jesus enters Jerusalem riding a donkey. Christians process with palm leaves woven as crosses to remember how the crowds placed palm leaves down for Jesus to enter on.
Maundy Thursday	Jesus' celebration of the Passover Festival in which he shares his body and blood in sharing the bread and wine in the Synoptic Gospels. In John's Gospel he washes his disciples' feet. The priest traditionally washes the congregation's feet to remember the importance of servant leadership.

22.1b Festivals & Celebration: Easter

IGCSE 2 Religious Studies

Key word	Definition
	EASTERTIDE
Easter Sunday	Celebrates the ('particular') resurrection of Jesus and looks forward to the general resurrection at the end time ('*eschaton*') when sin and death will be conquered at the second coming ('*parousia*') of Christ.
Easter Vigil	Service at dusk on Easter Sunday, in which a bonfire is lit and the Paschal candle is lit from the bonfire and processed into church.
Paschal candle	Easter candle that is typically large and decorated; 5 studs with incense inside are put in it to remember the 5 wounds of Christ.
Votive candles	Individual candles that are lit from the Paschal candle to show that Christians share in the life of God revealed in Christ.
Revelation 22	Description of Jesus as the 'alpha and omega', typically used to decorate the Paschal candle.
Ascension Day	40 days after Easter Sunday on which Jesus bodily ascended to heaven, celebrated with a communion of Bible readings and relevant hymns.
Pentecost	50 days after Easter Sunday and the last day of Eastertide. It celebrates the gift of the Holy Spirit to the apostles, allowing them to 'speak in tongues' and perform miracles. It marks the beginning of the authority of the church.
Acts 2	Apostles understand each other each in their own language
1 Corinthians 14	Speaking in tongues is also described as a direct communication with God that is incomprehensible to others.
Acts 3	Inspired by the Holy Spirit, St Peter was able to perform the miracle of healing a lame beggar.

Test yourself

(a) Outline **two** rituals associated with Easter. (4)
(b) Explain the history of the celebration of Easter. (6)
(c) "Easter is the most important Christian festival." Discuss.
Discuss this statement considering the arguments for and against.
  In your answer you should include:
  - reference to teachings
  - other (divergent) points of view – either within the religion or from other religions
  - your opinion/point of view using reasoned arguments
  - a balanced conclusion. (10)

2.2.2a Places of Pilgrimage: Bethlehem

REVISED

GENERIC SYLLABUS REQUIREMENTS
The importance of two named places of pilgrimage and their observances & traditions.

CHRISTIAN SYLLABUS REQUIREMENTS.
The importance of Bethlehem and its observances & traditions.

Significance of Bethlehem

REVISED

> **Key point**
>
> Joseph and Mary had to travel to Bethlehem for a Roman census and it is there that Mary gave birth to Jesus in a stable, as there was nowhere else to stay.

- Jesus' family lived in Nazareth, but there was a census (survey) being undertaken by the Roman Empire to establish who worked in each area. This required the surrounding population to travel to Bethlehem to be counted. As a result, Mary and her husband Joseph had to travel to Bethlehem even though Mary was pregnant.

- Bethlehem is approximately 70 miles from Nazareth so Joseph and Mary would have had a long and difficult journey. (Bethlehem is situated 5½ miles west of Jerusalem.)

- There was no room in Bethlehem for Mary and Joseph to stay since so many others were also needing to attend the census. Finally, Mary and Joseph found shelter in a stable. Mary gave birth in that stable and laid Jesus down in a manger (animals' eating trough).

- Bethlehem is prophesied as the birthplace of the Messiah or Christ (the 'anointed one', who is marked with oil as a leader) in Micah 5:2: 'But you, Bethlehem Ephrathah ['fruitful'], though you are small among the clans of Judah, but of you will come for me one who will be ruler over Israel, whose origins are from of old, from ancient times."

- Jesus' birth is seen to fulfil this prophesy.

- The birth of Jesus is also claimed to be the incarnation, in which the Trinitarian God (in the 'person' of the Son or Word) becomes a human: 'The Word became flesh and made his dwelling among us. We have seen his glory, the glory of the one and only Son, who came from the Father, full of grace and truth.' (John 1)

- Bethlehem is important for allowing Christians to identify with those in desperate situations similar to Mary and Joseph's - people forced from their homes (such as immigrants) or having children in poverty.

- Jesus' birth is also a sign of the miracle of childbirth - Christ's birth is a revelation of what St. Aquinas called the 'theological virtues' of 'faith, hope and love', which find their clearest expression in 1 Corinthians 13. This encourages us to see all birth as something transformative and inspiring, to be respected and cared for.

- Christian pilgrims travel to Bethlehem, particularly at Christmas time, to attend services in the Church of the Nativity, perhaps kissing the star that marks the place of Jesus' birth.

- Visiting the actual place in which Jesus was born allows pilgrims to experience their faith more historically.

Church of the Nativity

> **Key point**
>
> A church in Bethlehem built on the site of Jesus' birth.

- The Church of the Nativity is off 'Manger Square'. This is a city square in the centre of Bethlehem in Palestine, which commemorates Jesus' birth. Bethlehem's Christmas celebrations are focused there, with a giant Christmas tree crowning the square. Pilgrims sing Christmas carols there before midnight mass at the Church of the Nativity.
- The Church of the Nativity is the most important site in Bethlehem. The Emperor Constantine originally built the church in the 4thc. AD in the form of a basilica. The original church was destroyed in the 6th c. AD when the Byzantine Emperor crushed Samaritan revolts, but the church was rebuilt by Emperor Justinian shortly afterwards.
- The Church of the Nativity expanded over the centuries and today it covers approximately 12,000 square metres. It includes three different monasteries: one Greek Orthodox, one Armenian Apostolic, and one Roman Catholic.
- The Church of the Nativity is entered through a very low door called the "Door of Humility". The main Church is designed as a 'basilica'. Ssee 2.3.1: 'Places of Worship' for a discussion of church architecture).
- The Church's interior has remnants of mediaeval golden mosaics on its walls and underneath the stone floor there is still some of Emperor Constantine's original mosaic pavement (4thc. AD).
- Beneath the Church of the Nativity is the crypt (underground chapel or burial chamber), which is called the 'Grotto of the Nativity'.
- At the Grotto's eastern niche is the Altar of the Nativity, and under the altar is a 14-pointed silver star with the Latin inscription *'Hic De Virgine Maria Jesus Christus Natus Est – 1717'* ("Here Jesus Christ was born to the Virgin Mary" – 1717) [The date refers to when the inscription was added.] This is the exact place where Jesus is said to be born.
- Another section of the Church is the Grotto of the Manger, in which Mary is claimed to have laid down her baby Jesus in a manger.
- The underground passages of the Grotto of the Nativity connect to the neighbouring Church of St. Catherine of Alexandria.
- The different sections of the church are under the authority of different Christian denominations: Greek Orthodox, Armenian Apostolic and Roman Catholic.
- The Church of the Nativity was made a World Heritage Site in 2012. The rights of different denominations over different areas were decreed by Ottoman Sultan Osman III in 1757 and internationally ratified in Article 9 of the Treaty of Paris (1856).
- Due to the Roman Catholics following the Gregorian calendar and the Eastern Orthodox following the 'old' Julian calendar, the denominations celebrate Christmas on different day in the Church of the Nativity..

Recall the definitions ... quiz yourself both ways

Key word	Definition
Nazareth	Home town of Mary and Joseph
Census	Roman survey requiring Mary to travel to Bethlehem
Bethlehem	The place of pilgrimage for Jesus' birth
Church of the Nativity	The Church that celebrates the birth of Jesus
Emperor Constantine	Originally built the Church of the Nativity in 4th c. AD
Emperor Justinian	Rebuilt the Church of the Nativity in the 6th century AD after it had been destroyed by a Samaritan revolt.
Manger Square	Square in which the Church of the Nativity stands
Nativity Monasteries	Greek Orthodox, Armenian Apostolic & Roman Catholic
Door of Humility	Low door that grants access to Church of Nativity
Basilica	Church architectural style of Church of the Nativity, based upon a Roman public building used for court cases.
Grotto Chapel	The chapel in the Church of the Nativity's crypt
Altar of the nativity	An altar in the Eastern niche of the Chapel of the grotto beneath which is a 14-pointed star.
14-pointed star	Marks the place of Jesus' birth
Latin inscription	'Hic De Virgine Maria Jesus Christus Natus Est – 1717' ("Here Jesus Christ was born to the Virgin Mary" – 1717)
Grotto of the Manger	Chapel where Mary laid Jesus in a manger
St Catherine of Alexandria	Church united to the Church of the Nativity by underground tunnels.
World Heritage site	UNESCO makes Church of the Nativity such a site in 2012
Status Quo	Rights of different denominations to access the Church of the Nativity, agreed in Article 9 of the Treaty of Paris (1856).

Test yourself

(a) Outline **two** places of pilgrimage in Bethlehem. (4)
(b) Explain the significance of Bethlehem for Christians. (6)
(c) "The money spent on pilgrimages would be better spent on charity." Discuss.
Discuss this statement considering the arguments for and against.
   In your answer you should include:
   - reference to teachings
   - other (divergent) points of view – either within the religion or from other religions
   - your opinion/point of view using reasoned arguments
   - a balanced conclusion. (10)

2.2.2b Places of Pilgrimage: Jerusalem

REVISED ☐

GENERIC SYLLABUS REQUIREMENTS
The importance of two named places of pilgrimage and their observances & traditions.

CHRISTIAN SYLLABUS REQUIREMENTS.
The importance of Jerusalem and its observances & traditions.

Significance of Jerusalem

REVISED ☐

> **Key point**
>
> Ancient capital of Israel, which includes the Garden of Gethsemane, the *via dolorosa* and the Church of the Holy Sepulchre commemorating Jesus' crucifixion & resurrection.

- Jerusalem is an important place of pilgrimage for Christians, just as it is for Jews and Muslims.

- For the Jews, Jerusalem is the site of the 'promised land', given to Abraham in Genesis 15: 'To your descendants I give this land, from the Wadi of Egypt to the great river, the Euphrates.' It is also the site of the sacred temple of Solomon, which has been repeatedly demolished and rebuilt. It was last destroyed in 70AD under the Roman Empire and never rebuilt.

- For Muslims, Jerusalem is also important. Muslims used to pray towards Jerusalem before finally praying towards Mecca. In the 7th c. AD, the Muslim Umayyad Caliph Abd al-Malik ibn Marwan conquered Jerusalem and ordered the construction of an Islamic shrine on the site of the Jewish temple; this is the Dome of the Rock, which still stands today. The al-Aqsa Mosque, which is also still standing, was built in the original Jewish Temple's courtyard.

- For Christians, Jerusalem is the most important holy site for most Christians. It marks the crucifixion, resurrection and ascension of Jesus. Crusades were fought from the 11th to 13th centuries AD to win back Jerusalem from Muslim rule. Nevertheless, some Christians do not see pilgrimage sites to be very important, emphasising instead what the 'new life' of 'grace' that Jesus has revealed to us, rather than be overly concerned with the historical sites in which this occurred.

- Christians believe that Jesus visited Jerusalem at Passover time and spent the week leading up to his death there. Christian pilgrims visit Jerusalem therefore, to remember key events in Jesus' final week, known as Holy Week. Places that Christian pilgrims might visit include the following:

Garden of Gethsemane

> **Key point**
>
> Garden in which Jesus prayed and was arrested.

- The Garden of Gethsemane – this is believed to be where Jesus prayed before he was arrested by the Romans and put to death.
- Jesus had asked his disciples to stay awake and pray with him, but they fell asleep even though it was Jesus' most desperate time of soul searching. This allows Christians to reflect upon the solitude of anxious soul searching.
- Jesus prayed to God in the garden: 'Father, if you are willing, take this cup of suffering away from me. Yet not my will, but yours be done.' (Luke 22) Jesus accepted his fate without complaining, inspiring Christians to similarly fulfil their responsibilities to God.
- Judas betrayed Jesus with a kiss in the garden of Gethsemane so as to indicate to the Jewish authorities who Jesus was so that they could arrest him. Jesus said: 'Judas, are you betraying the Son of Man with a kiss?' (Luke 22) This allows Christians to look for a higher purpose, even when they are tempted to simply look to their own purposes and defend themselves.
- In the garden, the disciples tried to protect Jesus against those arresting him, and Simon Peter cut off the ear of one of the soldiers. Jesus said, 'Those who live by the sword shall die by the sword.' (John 18) This allows Christians to see even those who do them violence as belonging to God's plan.

The Church of the Holy Sepulchre

> **Key point**
>
> Church marking the place where Jesus was crucified, entombed & resurrected.

- Some believe that the Church of the Holy Sepulchre is built where Jesus was crucified, as well as his place of entombment. (Others believe the Garden Tomb, outside Jerusalem's city walls, is the actual place which marks the site of the death and resurrection of Jesus.)
- The church includes:
  1. The Stone of the Anointing on which Jesus was prepared to be entombed.
  2. Chapel of the 3 Marys (Mary the mother of Jesus, Mary the sister of the mother of Jesus and Mary Magdalene - all of whom were at the foot of the cross).
  3. The Rotunda – place of entombment of Jesus; Jesus was buried in the tomb of Joseph of Arimathea (a follower of Jesus who is not to be confused with the father of Jesus (though not the biological father since Jesus' father is God) Joseph.
  4. A number of different denominational chapels exist around the Rotunda such as the Syrian chapel and the Coptic chapel. Underneath the Coptic chapel, there is Jesus' burial tomb donated by Joseph of Arimathea.
  5. The chapel of Mary Magdalene, where Mary saw the resurrected Jesus but didn't recognise him until he spoke to her, originally confusing him with a gardener.

6. The Franciscan chapel in which Jesus was whipped and tied to a column.
7. The stone of Golgotha is the rock on which Jesus was crucified. Pilgrims touch the stone to better understand Christ's sacrifice.
8. Underneath the Stone of Golgotha, there is the Chapel of Adam, recognising that Jesus is the new Adam, atoning for Adam's "original sin".

Via Dolorosa

REVISED

Key point

Latin for "painful path" and is the name for the road on which Jesus had to carry his own cross for crucifixion.

- Via Dolorosa - this is a special route that Christian pilgrims walk from the outskirts of Jerusalem to the Church of the Holy Sepulchre, especially on Good Friday. It is believed to be the very path that Jesus took carrying his cross on the way to his crucifixion.
- The 'stations of the cross' are 14 events that happened while Jesus was carrying his cross. Meditating upon them allows Catholics to imaginatively share in Jesus' last journey on the 'via dolorosa'. if they are not capable of actually visiting Jerusalem.

Church of the Ascension

REVISED

Key point

Church that marks the place where Jesus ascended bodily to heaven.

- Church of the Ascension – this is said to mark the site of the Ascension, when Jesus rose into Heaven forty days after his resurrection. There is a stone inside the Church, believed to be imprinted with his footsteps.
- Having conquered sin and death in his resurrection, Jesus bodily ascends to the Father

Recall the definitions ... quiz yourself both way

Key word	Definition	TESTED
Jerusalem	Capital of Israel and the place of Jesus' crucifixion, resurrection and ascension.	
Genesis 15	Jerusalem and Israel are seen as the promised land granted to Abraham	
Islam	Muslims used to pray towards Jerusalem before this was changed to Mecca.	
Dome of the Rock	Caliph ibn Marwan conquered Jerusalem and ordered the construction of this Islamic shrine on the site of the Jewish temple	
Crusades	Fought from the 11th to 13th centuries AD to win back Jerusalem from Muslim rule.	

22b Places of Pilgrimage: Jerusalem

Key word	Definition
Passover	Passover was a major festival in Jerusalem, celebrating that the angel of death 'passed over' the Jewish houses when killing the first-born children of the Egyptians.
Garden of Gethsemane	Where Jesus prayed before he was arrested by the Jewish authorities and taken to King Herod.
Jesus' prayers in that garden	'Father, if you are willing, take this cup of suffering away from me. Yet not my will, but yours be done.' (Luke 22)
Jesus to Judas	'Judas, are you betraying the Son of Man with a kiss?' (Luke 22)
Simon Peter	Cut off the ear of one of the soldiers arresting Jesus
Church of the Holy Sepulchre	A Jerusalem church, which celebrates where Jesus was crucified, buried and resurrected.
Philip D'Auberny.	Crusader buried outside the Church of the Holy Sepulchre.
Chapel of the 3 Marys	Mary the mother of Jesus, Mary her sister and Mary Magdalene
Stone of the anointing	Where Jesus was prepared to be entombed.
Rotunda	A chapel commemorating Jesus' entombment in Joseph of Arimathea's tomb
Chapel of Mary Magdalene	Chapel commemorating Mary's first witnessing the resurrection.
Franciscan chapel	Remembers Jesus being whipped and tied to a column
Stone of Golgotha	The rock on which Jesus was crucified
Atonement	Jesus dying on the cross to save us from our sins
Particular Resurrection	Jesus conquering sin and death by rising from the dead, looking forward to the end time ('*eschaton*') when sin and death will be finally conquered.
Via Dolorosa	Path of sorrows on which Jesus had to carry his cross.
Stations of the Cross	14 events that Catholics recollect as they try to understand Jesus' sacrifice as he carried his cross on the *Via Dolorosa*.

Test yourself

(a) Outline **two** reasons for going on pilgrimage. (4)
(b) Explain the traditions and observances of pilgrims in Jerusalem. (6)
(c) "Jerusalem is Christianity's most significant site of pilgrimage."
Discuss this statement considering the arguments for and against.
  In your answer you should include:
- reference to teachings
- other (divergent) points of view – either within the religion or from other religions
- your opinion/point of view using reasoned arguments
- a balanced conclusion. (10)

IGCSE 2 Religious Studies

Churches of the Nativity & Holy Sepulchre

REVISED ☐

CHURCH OF THE NATIVITY: BETHLEHEM

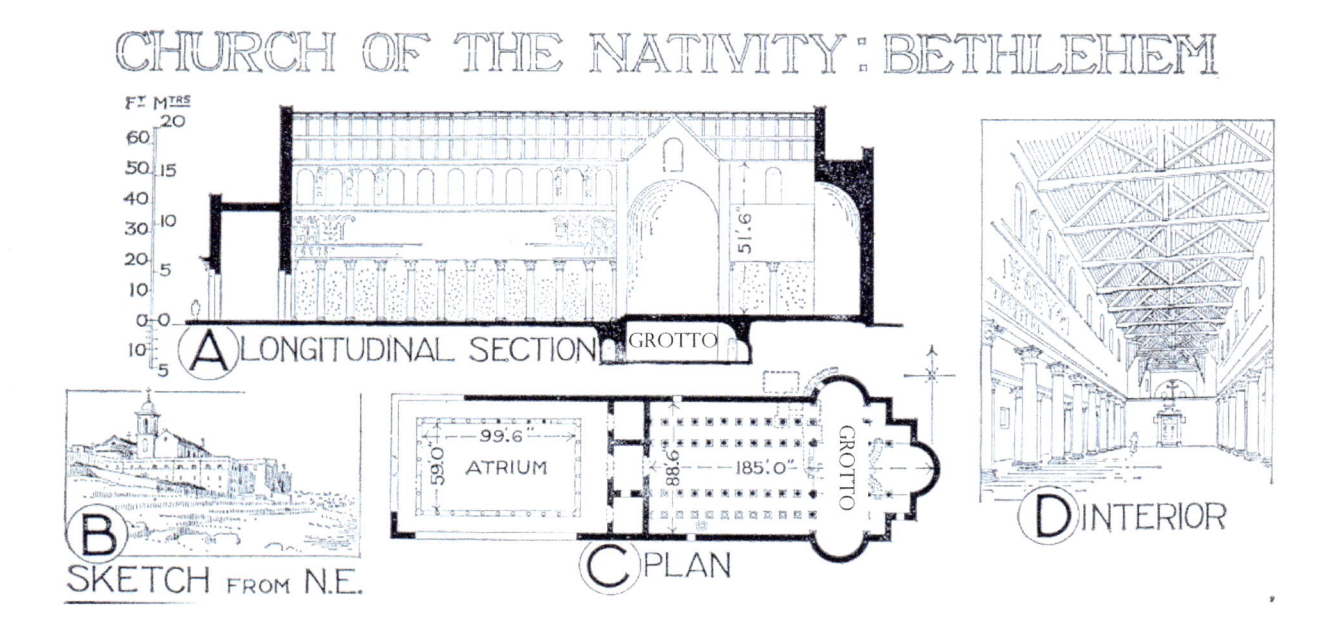

A. LONGITUDINAL SECTION — GROTTO
B. SKETCH FROM N.E.
C. PLAN — ATRIUM 59'0" × 99'6", 185'0", GROTTO
D. INTERIOR

- For a tour of the Church of the Nativity, see "The Church of the Nativity" from Drive Thru History®: The Gospels (https://www.youtube.com/watch?v=7ZZElyEclWk)

CHURCH OF THE HOLY SEPULCHRE: JERUSALEM

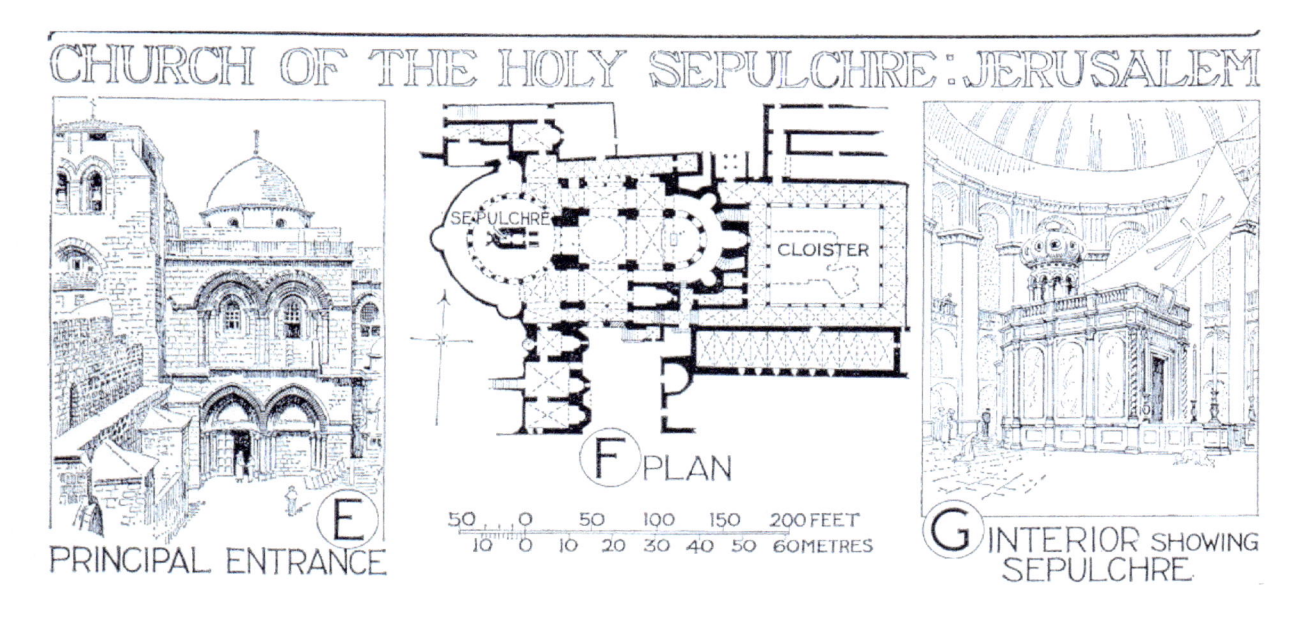

E. PRINCIPAL ENTRANCE
F. PLAN — SEPULCHRE, CLOISTER
G. INTERIOR SHOWING SEPULCHRE

- For a 3D-journey, tracing the Church of the Holy Sepulchre back through history to its being the site of Jesus' crucifixion & resurrection, see "Holy Sepulchre, a 3D-journey back in time" at https://www.youtube.com/watch?v=25aqkcrzSyQ

IGCSE 2 Religious Studies

Cross-section of the Church of the Holy Sepulchre

REVISED

The "edicule" contains the flat stone on which Christ's body was laid

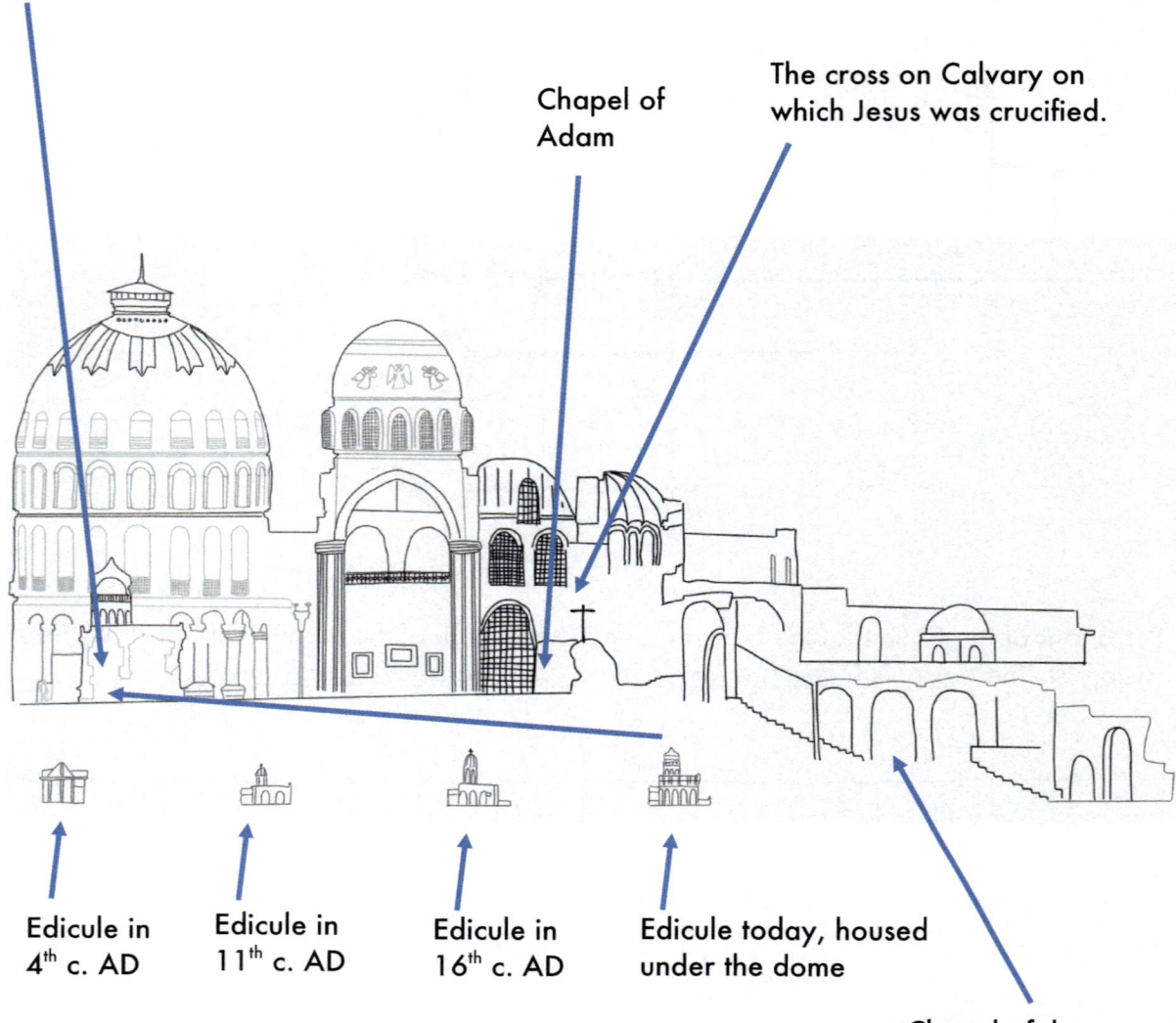

Chapel of Adam

The cross on Calvary on which Jesus was crucified.

Edicule in 4th c. AD

Edicule in 11th c. AD

Edicule in 16th c. AD

Edicule today, housed under the dome

Chapel of the Finding of the Cross; legend says that Constantine's mother found parts of the Cross of Christ here.

222b Places of Pilgrimage: Jerusalem

70 IGCSE 2 Religious Studies

222c Places of Pilgrimage: Vatican City

REVISED

GENERIC SYLLABUS REQUIREMENTS
The importance of one other place of pilgrimage and its observances & traditions.

CHRISTIAN SYLLABUS REQUIREMENTS.
The importance of Vatican City and its observances & traditions for Christianity and, in particular, the denomination of Roman Catholicism.

History of Vatican City

REVISED

> **Key point**
>
> Vatican City is an independent country in Rome. It is seat of government of the Roman Catholic Church and includes St. Peter's Basilica.

- Peter is regarded as the supreme apostle for Roman Catholicism and the first Pope (Bishop of Rome and supreme authority in 'Roman Catholicism). God passed his authority to Peter through Jesus: 'You are Peter, and on this rock I will build my church.' (Matthew 16)
- Tradition says that after Pentecost in Jerusalem, when the apostles received the Holy Spirit as described in Acts 2, Peter went to Rome.
- After much of Rome was destroyed in a fire in 64AD, Emperor Nero made scapegoats of the Christians, and the apostle Peter was crucified on Vatican Hill.
- The Roman Emperor Constantine I declared religious toleration for Christianity in Rome in the Edict of Milan in 313AD.
- Following an attack by Saracen pirates in 846AD, Pope Leo IV ordered the construction of a wall to protect this centre of the Christian faith.
- Completed in 852AD, the 39-foot-tall wall enclosed an area covering the current Vatican territory and the Borgo district.
- The Papal Court moved to France in 1309, but then returned to Rome in 1377.
- Popes traditionally controlled regional territories known as the Papal States, but in 1870 the unified Italian government included all these states in the Italian nation.
- Vatican City was established as a sovereign nation with the signing of the Lateran Pacts in 1929 by the then-prime minister Mussolini.
- Vatican City is the smallest country in the world, with a landmass of just under 1/2 square kilometre.
- The Vatican has its own banking and telephone systems, post office, pharmacy, newspaper and radio and television stations.
- Its 600 citizens include the Swiss Guard, who dress in traditional clothes, dating back to their first protecting the pope in 1506.

IGCSE 2 Religious Studies

St Peter's Basilica

> **Key point**
>
> The largest church in the world, built on the site of St. Peter's crucifixion in Rome.

- The third pope Anacletus (1st c. AD) – built an oratory (a small chapel for private worship) over St Peter's tomb.
- In 337AD, Constantine the Great built St. Peter's Basilica on the site of St. Peter's tomb.
- Pope Julius II demolished the 1,200-year-old St. Peter's Basilica and in 1506 commissioned the architect Donato Bramante to create the largest and most impressive religious building in the world. Completed in 1626, St Peter's Basilica stands 452 feet tall and with an area of 5½ acres.
- There are over a hundred tombs under St. Peter's Basilica, including almost all of the Popes.
- Michelangelo's Pieta (a marble sculpture of Mary grieving over the body of Jesus after the crucifixion) is just within the entrance.
- A large piece of the true cross is enclosed in one of the four pillars facing the high altar.
- In the central nave is a 13th century statue of the seated apostle Peter; one foot has been worn thin from many thousands of pilgrims touching it.
- The pope regularly celebrates mass (communion) in St Peter's, allowing pilgrims to share in the body and blood of Christ through the authority of St Peter's spiritual successor.
- Outside the basilica is St Peter's Square – an impressive walkway through columns. On Wednesdays, the Pope addresses the gathered pilgrims in the square to speak to them.

The Sistine Chapel

> **Key point**
>
> A chapel in the Vatican whose ceiling is decorated by Michelangelo.

- In the 1470s, Pope Sixtus IV began work on the Sistine Chapel, which includes frescoes by the Renaissance artists Botticelli and Perugino on the walls.
- In 1508, Pope Julius II commissioned Michelangelo to paint the Sistine Chapel ceiling. This is widely acknowledged to be of the greatest artistic achievements in history.
- The ceiling powerfully summarises the key teachings of the faith, allowing pilgrims to experience those teachings vividly and powerfully through Michelangelo's art.
- The Sistine chapel now functions as the papal conclave – the site in which a new pope is chosen by Cardinals (Bishops who are authorised to choose the next pope). Pilgrims can visit the area in which the sacred act of apostolic succession occurs.

Recall the definitions ... quiz yourself both ways

Key word	Definition
St Peter	Claimed to be the first pope and called by Jesus the 'rock upon which I shall build my church.' (Matthew 16)
Death of St Peter	Martyred when the Roman Emperor Nero blamed the Christians for the burning of Rome in 64AD, crucifying Peter.
Anacletus	Pope who built an oratory over St Peter's tomb in the 1st century AD
Edict of Milan	Emperor Constantine I declared tolerance for Christianity in 313AD.
St Peter's Basilica	In 337AD, Constantine I built St. Peter's Basilica above St. Peter's tomb.
Pope Julius II	In 1506, authorised a new St. Peter's Basilica, which was finished in 1626. The building is 452 feet tall with an area of 5½ acres
Michelangelo's Pieta	A marble sculpture of Mary grieving over the body of Jesus after the crucifixion, which is just within the entrance
True cross	Enclosed in one of the four huge pillars facing the high altar.
Apostle Peter's statue	13th century statue of which one foot has been worn thin from many thousands of pilgrims touching it.
Avignon Papacy	In 1309, the Papacy moved to France but then returned to Rome in 1377.
Sistine Chapel	In the 1470s, Pope Sixtus IV began work on the Sistine Chapel, which includes frescoes by the Renaissance artists Botticelli and Perugino
Michelangelo	In 1508, Pope Julius II commissioned Michelangelo to paint the Sistine Chapel ceiling
Papal Conclave	The meeting of Cardinals in the Sistine Chapel to decide the next pope.
Lateran Pacts	In 1929, Vatican City became a sovereign nation as agreed by the then-prime minister Mussolini.
Swiss Guard	Still in traditional clothes, they first started protecting the pope in 1506

TESTED

Test yourself

Done

(a) Outline **two** reasons to not go on pilgrimage. (4)

(b) Explain the significance of a Christian place of pilgrimage other than Bethlehem and Jerusalem. (6)

(c) "There are more important pilgrimage sites than Bethlehem or Jerusalem."
Discuss this statement considering the arguments for and against.
   In your answer you should include:
   - reference to teachings
   - other (divergent) points of view – either within the religion or from other religions
   - your opinion/point of view using reasoned arguments
   - a balanced conclusion. (10)

IGCSE 2 Religious Studies

Vatican City virtual tours

> **Vatican**
>
> A map of the independent country "Vatican City" in Rome, which includes the largest church in the world, St. Peter's Basilica. Just north of the church is the Sistine Chapel. 3D virtual tours can be found on the following links.

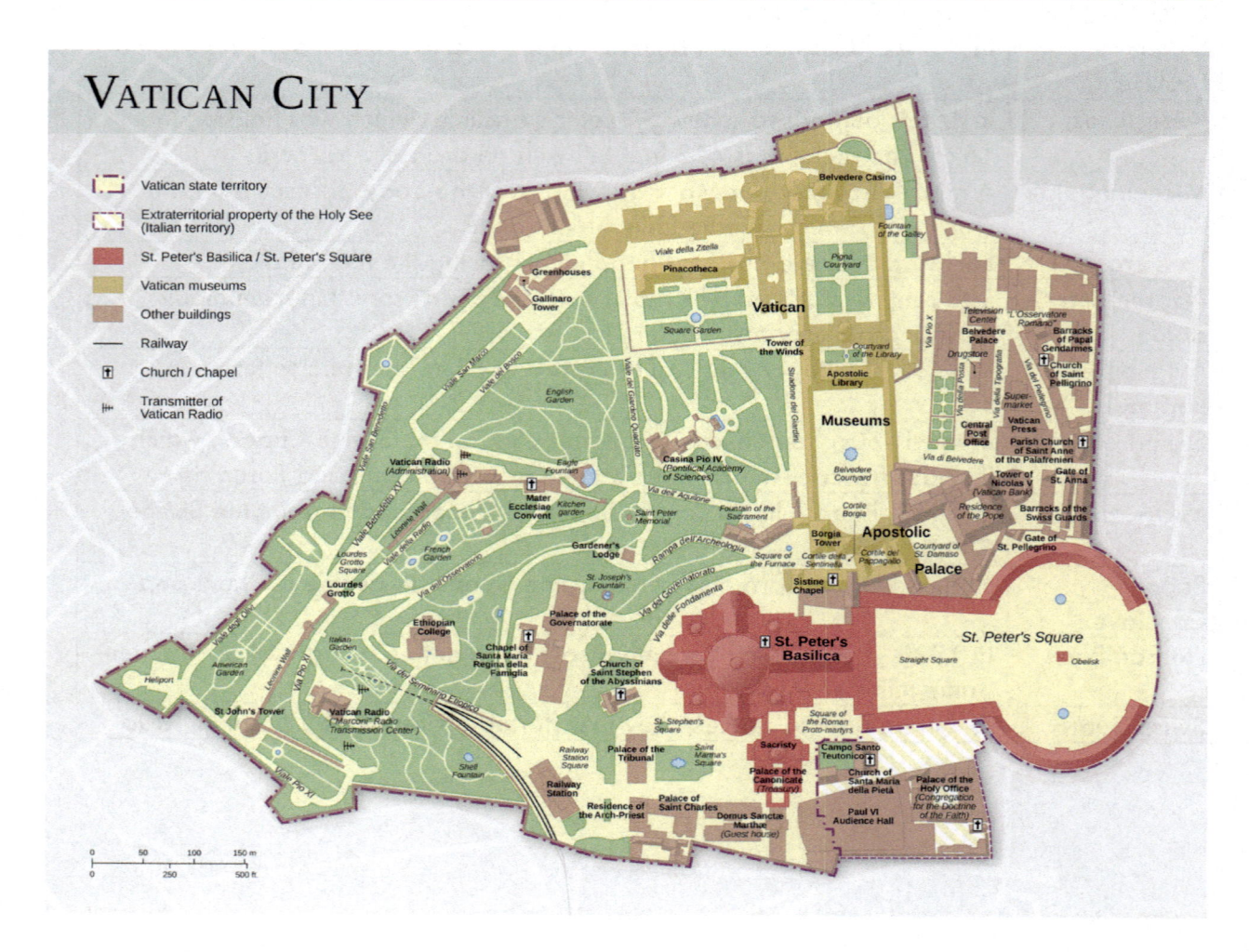

An interactive virtual tour of St. Peter's Basilica
https://www.vatican.va/various/basiliche/san_pietro/vr_tour/index-en.html

An interactive virtual tour of the Sistine Chapel
https://www.museivaticani.va/content/museivaticani/en/collezioni/musei/tour-virtuali-elenco.html

2.3 Worship & Practice

Topic 2.3.1a Places of Worship: Catholicism

REVISED ☐

GENERIC SYLLABUS
The design and purpose of regional, national or international places of public worship, focused on their internal & external appearances & the status of such buildings in the religion.

CHRISTIAN SYLLABUS
The contrasting design and purpose of two Christian denominations' local places of worship, focused on their internal & external appearances. The historical and contemporary importance of their design. The use of such buildings today and their status in the religion.

Catholic church's external appearance: its history

REVISED ☐

> **Key point**
>
> Development of Catholic churches from original "house churches" through the two-room church model (starting in the 4thc AD) to more inclusive church buildings (post-Vatican 2 of 20th c AD).

- The word 'church' can describe both the Christian community and its place of worship.
- In the first three centuries, Christianity was illegal and so Christians typically worshiped in private houses called 'house churches'; e.g., the house of Aquila and Priscilla. (1 Corinthians 16)
- In the Battle of Milvian Bridge in 312AD, the Constantine 1 became the new Emperor of Rome. He was a Christian and, in the Edict of Milan of 313AD, legalised Christianity.
- Christian churches were then built based on the Roman basilica rather than the Roman temple, which did not allow for people to gather inside. The Roman basilica was a large public building typically situated on the town's forum (square) in which many public functions were performed. It was rectangular in shape and included a central nave (central section in which people could sit) and a clerestory (windows towards the top section of the building to let light in).
- Another Roman building that influenced the building of Catholic Churches was the Roman Mausoleum. This was a square or circular domed structure inside which was a sarcophagus (a carved structure commemorating and containing someone who is dead). The Christian altar was built similar to a sarcophagus and over it was an apse (dome structure).
- This was placed at the East end of the church so as to associate Christ's death and resurrection, celebrated at the altar, with the rising sun for as Jesus says, 'I am the light of the world' (John 8).

IGCSE 2 Religious Studies

- With time, the altar was placed on a raised 'dais' (platform) called a 'bema' (elevated sanctuary) to emphasise the dignity of the ritual of communion.
- The 'bema' came to project out in both directions from the rectangular building to form a 'transept', making the building cross-shaped.
- With the rise of monasteries (monks funded by the people) a 'two-room' church developed, with the clerics (priests and monks) occupying the chancel (the sanctuary area housing the altar) and the congregation occupying the nave.
- These 'two rooms' came to be partitioned by a 'rood screen', which was typically a wooden partition.
- In the 10th and 11th centuries AD, churches started to be built in stone in northern Europe, and these churches still survive – the older wooden ones have perished. The architecture emphasised strength and solidity to emphasise the eternity of God.
- In the 12th century AD, the Gothic style of church architecture developed. It employed long tall columns, large stained-glass windows made possible by flying buttresses (supports to hold up the walls now that it includes so many windows). The churches employed artistry to great effect, its stained glass windows illustrating stories in the Bible and its statues celebrating Biblical characters and saints. The figures are typically elongated so as to emphasise their spirituality rather than their physicality.
- In the 16th century AD, break-away churches arose called 'Protestant' since each of these different churches protested against Catholic corruption. They typically rejected the artistry of the Catholic church, focusing on the teaching of scripture according to Martin Luther's principle of *'sola scriptura'*: scripture alone is necessary for salvation. The Catholic Counter-Reformation responded to this challenge by emphasising the centrality of art for faith in their Baroque churches, which were theatrical in their presentations of the teachings of the faith.
- In the 20th century AD, Pope John 23rd called the 2nd Vatican Council to change traditional Catholic worship. Meeting from 1959 to 1962, the Council agreed to change worship. One of the reforms was to make worship more inclusive: worship no longer needed to be performed in the universal language of Latin but could be performed in the local language. The priest no longer faced East when performing the eucharist towards the altar, but now stood behind the altar to face the congregation. The Catholic Church also started to build some of its churches in the 'round' with the altar at the centre and the congregation sitting around it. This was the case with the Liverpool Metropolitan Church, started in 1962 (the ending of the 2nd Vatican Council) and completed in 1967.
- Given the historic buildings of the church, there are therefore many different styles of Catholic Church – some dating back to the 4th century AD such as the Archbasilica of Saint John Lateran, founded by Constantine the Great after the Edict of Milan tolerating Christianity in 313AD. There are the soaring Gothic churches following the Abbey Church of Saint Denis in the 12th century AD. The Mother Church of the Society of Jesus (Jesuits), built in Rome in the 16th century AD, is the first of the Baroque churches. There are also churches built in the round such as the Liverpool Metropolitan Church of 1962 in accordance with Vatican 2 (1962-7).
- All of the churches are characterised by a sense of permanence and a sense of dignity however, indicating how Catholics share in the eternal tradition of the Catholic church.

Dome as architectural origin of apse over altar

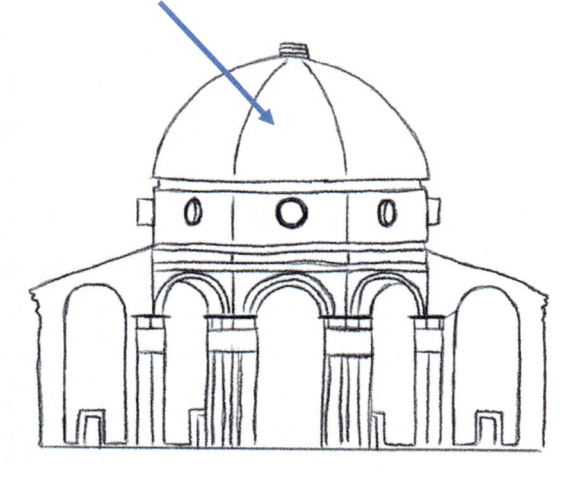

Sarcophagus

Roman Mausoleum

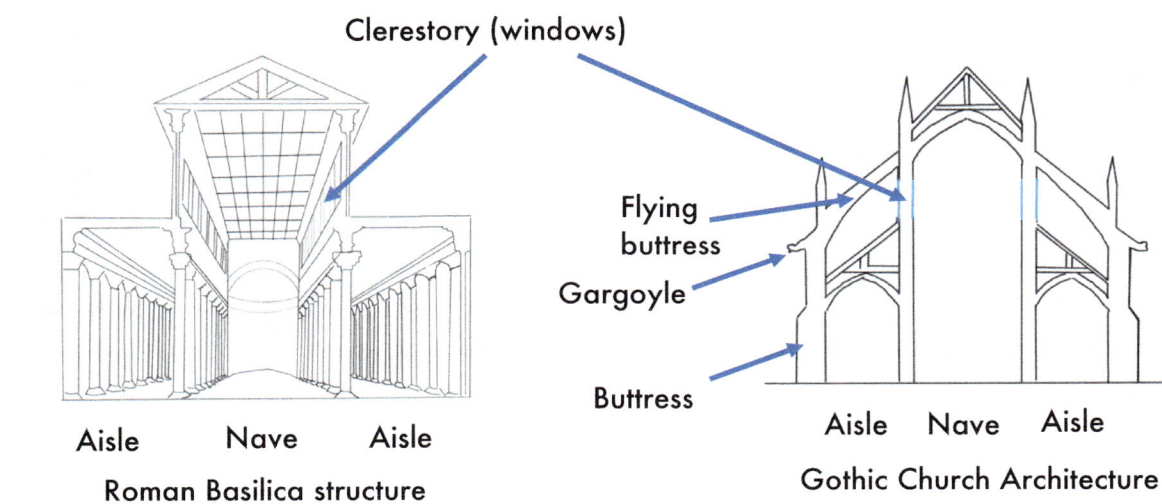

Clerestory (windows)

Flying buttress

Gargoyle

Buttress

Aisle Nave Aisle
Roman Basilica structure

Aisle Nave Aisle
Gothic Church Architecture

Liverpool Metropolitan Cathedral outside & floorplan on right

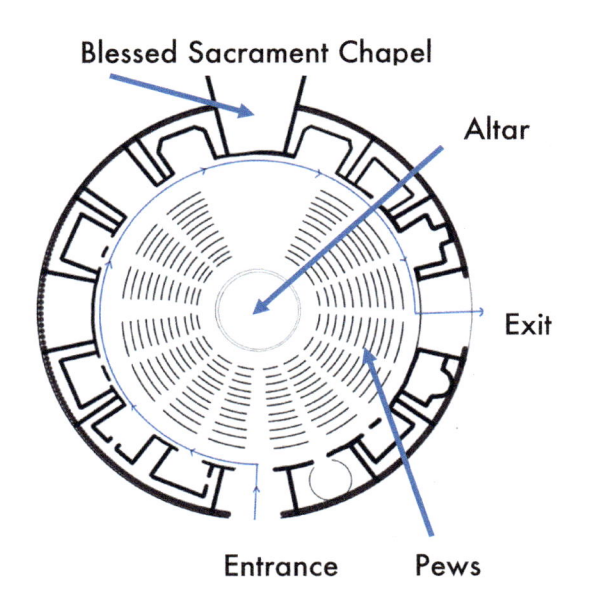

Blessed Sacrament Chapel

Altar

Exit

Entrance Pews

IGCSE 2 Religious Studies

Catholic church's internal appearance & its use

> **Key point**
>
> Features to be found in most Catholic Churches & their uses.

- Catholic churches involve a number of features for coming to know God.

- The altar is the sacrificial table on which Jesus' sacrifice is commemorated. When the priest 'consecrates' the bread by saying Jesus' words: 'Take eat this is my body given for you' the bread is said to 'transubstantiate' into the body of Christ – take on the nature of Christ's body even though its appearances ('accidents') remain those of bread. Similarly, when the priest 'consecrates' the wine by saying Jesus' words: 'This is my blood of the new covenant, which is shed for you and for many for the forgiveness of sins' the wine is said to 'transubstantiate' into the blood of Christ. By sharing in the body and blood of Christ, Christians share in the life of God on earth revealed in Christ. The wine is consecrated in a beautiful cup called a chalice; this is typically silver.

- The 'tabernacle' is a beautifully decorated safe that is typically placed on or beside the altar. The consecrated bread and wine that have not been consumed (i.e., eaten or drunk) are placed in this safe so as to protect the body and blood of Christ. These consecrated 'elements' can be used to give 'home communion' to the sick who cannot attend church.

- Beside the altar there is the Paschal Candle, which is an ornate candle which is lit during the Easter vigil at a bonfire before being brought into the church on Easter Sunday. This candle represents Jesus as the 'light of the world' (John 8) and it is used to light other candles during the Easter service and during baptisms to show how Christians share in the light of God through Christ.

- Above the altar there is typically a chancel stained-glass window depicting central events in the life of Jesus such as his crucifixion and resurrection, showing how people are saved by Jesus' sacrifice and are promised new life when they accept that sacrifice and so overcome sin and death through God's grace.

- Above the altar there is also typically a crucifix – a statue with Christ hanging on the cross indicating Christ's suffering for our sins through his sacrifice for us, allowing us 'atonement' or reconciliation with God.

- Inside the sanctuary, there is also typically a 'sanctuary candle' which is permanently lit, and all the candles are lit from this candle indicating how the light of Christ is eternal and passed on.

- Beside the altar, there is the priest's chair which is typically grand to indicate that the priest shares in God's authority through the power of apostolic succession. For Jesus says, 'you are Peter, and on this rock I will build my church.' (Matthew 16). Just as Jesus passes his authority on to Peter, that authority is passed down through the church to the priest celebrating the eucharist and forgiving sins: for as Jesus says, 'Whoever's sins you forgive, they are forgiven them.' (John 20)

- There is typically an 'altar rail' or in more traditional churches a 'rood screen' [see above] dividing the chancel/sanctuary from the nave. On passing through this rail, people are coming closer to the mystery or 'sacrament' of God's revelation.

IGCSE 2 Religious Studies

- Just outside the altar rail there is typically a lectern from which the Bible is read. This belongs to the 'liturgy of the word', which precedes the 'liturgy of the sacrament' which involves the eucharist being performed in the sanctuary.

- Between the sanctuary and the nave there are typically choir stalls. The choir typically sings sacred sections of the 'mass' (communion) such as the 'gloria' (giving glory to God at the beginning of communion), the *'kyrie'* (a prayer of purification including the words *'Lord have mercy'*) and the *'sanctus and benedictus'* (a prayer of holiness performed just before the rite (ritual) of consecrating the 'elements' (bread and wine). Psalms are also typically sung.

- In the nave, there is also the pulpit, which is typically an elevated area in which the priest gives the sermon, highlighting the importance of God's eternal word in the everyday life of the congregation.

- In the nave, there are also typically votive candles for the congregation to light when saying personal prayers for their loved ones.

- The congregation sit in pews (fixed benches) in more traditional churches. These are typically facing the altar, but in monasteries they face inwards so that the congregation sit facing each other.

- Along the walls of the nave, there are often pictures of the 14 stations of the cross-marking Jesus' crucifixion. These focus on key events when Jesus carried his cross through the 'via dolorosa' (a road called the way of suffering) prior to his execution.

- Towards the door, there is often a 'font'. The priest blesses the water in this prior to pouring the water over the head of an infant or adult in the sacrament of baptism.

- There might also be a confessional – traditionally, these were boxes with a screen through which the congregation would confess their sins to a priest, who would then offer God's forgiveness ('absolution') according to John 20: 'Whoever's sins you forgive, they are forgiven.' To receive this absolution, the believer needs to perform a 'penance' ((ation to demonstrate that they are sorry for their sins). In more modern Catholic Churches, they are meeting rooms for a face-to-face discussion.

- Outside the door there is a 'stoup', which is a small basin of water. The congregation often dip their finger in this water and make the sign of the cross when entering the church so as to recognise that they are entering holy ground. They might also say a prayer such as 'Wash me clean of my iniquity and cleanse me from my sin' (1 John 9).

- There is often a church hall attached to a church to allow for social gatherings. These are often leased out to local clubs for community projects (e.g., the Scouts).

Local place of worship

> **Key point**
>
> The syllabus refers to "local places of worship of any two Christian denominations" and so you should be able to name & describe yours, using the above information to help.

- Research your local Catholic place of worship. Ensure that you can discuss the external and internal appearance of your local Catholic Church, drawing upon the traditional features discussed above.

- For example, St Gregory's is the local Catholic Church in Cheltenham. You might also use your local Anglo-Catholic church. Anglo-Catholicism is a branch of the Church of England that is loyal to the ancient traditions of the church. For example, All Saints is the local Anglo-Catholic church in Cheltenham and includes all of the above features of a Catholic church.

- For example, All Saints, Cheltenham is in the shape of a basilica, and some of its architectural features are presented below.

St Stephen's Church (Catholic building)

REVISED ☐

> **Key point**
> The Catholic architectural features of St Stephen's Church, Cheltenham. Pictures identify features located in the floorplan of the building.

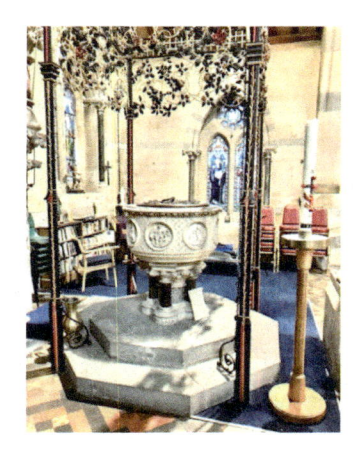

Font & Paschal Candle

Pulpit

Rood screen & apse over altar

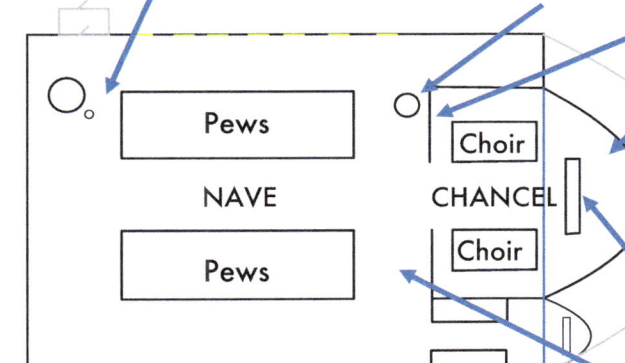

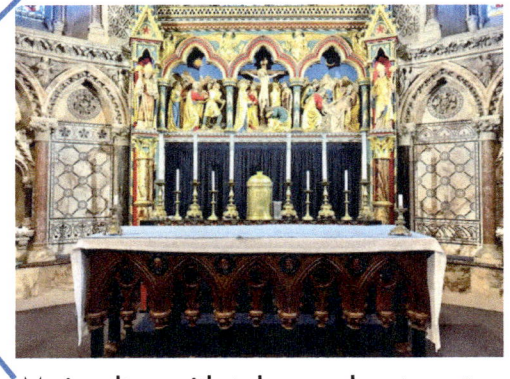

Main altar with tabernacle at centre

Lectern

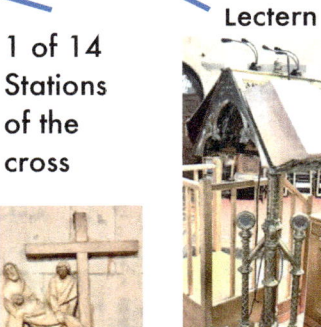

Statue of Mary with votive candles

1 of 14 Stations of the cross

St Stephen's Church exterior

IGCSE 2 Religious Studies   81

Recall the definitions ... quiz yourself both ways

231a Places of Worship: Catholicism

Key word	Definition
Church	Can refer to either Christians or the building in which they worship
House Churches	Christians meeting in private houses from the 1st to 3rd centuries AD when Christianity was illegal in the Roman empire.
Edict of Milan	In 313AD, Emperor Constantine 1 declared Christianity to be legal, allowing Christian churches to be built.
Roman basilica	Roman rectangular building in which public functions were performed and which became the basis for the design of churches.
Roman Mausoleum	Square or circular domed structure with a sarcophagus inside which became the basis for the design of the apse over the altar in churches.
Sarcophagus	Carved structure containing someone who is dead
Apse	A roof that is a hemi-sphere, built over the altar.
Dais	A low platform for a lectern or the priest's seat
Bema	The raised area of the sanctuary
Two rooms church	The clergy (priests and monks) came to be separated from the congregation by separating the sanctuary from the nave.
Rood screen	Wooden partition dividing the sanctuary from the nave
Reformation	Protestants in the 16th century AD, following the monk Martin Luther, rejected the splendour of church buildings in favour of focusing on the teaching of scripture ('*sola scriptura*').
Counter-reformation	The Catholic Church defended the splendour of Catholic worship in its 'baroque' churches such as the Mother Church of the Society of Jesus (Jesuits), built in Rome in the 16th century AD.
Vatican 2	'Ecumenical' Council of Catholic Bishops meeting in 1962-7 to agree reforms of Catholic worship. ['Ecumenical' does not mean here inter-denominational, but concerns broad agreement amongst Catholic leaders.]
Liverpool Metropolitan Church	Church built in the round in accordance with reforms of Vatican 2, which no longer saw the clergy to be distinct from the congregation (behind a rood screen), but as central to the congregation.
Altar	Sacrificial table used by Christians to commemorate Jesus' sacrificial death to 'atone' for our sins.
Atonement	Establishes peace through paying the price of sin
'Elements'	Bread and wine prior to consecration
Consecration	The priests' saying Christ's words at the Last Supper over the bread and wine so that they become the body and blood of Christ.
Transubstantiation	At the consecration, the bread takes on the essential nature of Christ's body and the wine takes on the essential nature of Christ's blood, but their appearance as bread and wine remain unchanged.
Tabernacle	Beautiful safe in which the body and blood of Christ is stored if it is not immediately consumed.
Paschal candle	Elaborate candle lit at the Easter Vigil and held near the altar in the sanctuary. It is used to light baptismal candles to show how Christians share in the light of Christ.

IGCSE 2 Religious Studies

Key word	Definition
Chancel	The most sacred area of a church in which the altar stands.
Stained glass	Windows in church depicting Biblical scenes through coloured glass
Crucifix	Statue of Jesus hanging on the cross, reminding the people of Christ's atoning for their sins.
Sanctuary candle	A candle that typically hangs from the ceiling and is permanently lit indicating the eternity of the light of Christ.
Priest's chair	A seat in the sanctuary that is typically elevated to indicate the dignity of the office of priesthood.
Altar rail	Rail that separates the chancel from the nave. (In older churches this became the 'rood screen'.
Choir stalls	The seats of the choir, typically with raised platforms to hold music.
Pews	Fixed benches in churches
Stations of the Cross	Pictures on the wall of the nave, marking 14 events focused on the crucifixion and Jesus' carrying his cross on the *via dolorosa* road.
Font	Contains water and is used for the rite of baptism, allowing the priest to pour blessed water on the infant's or adult's forehead.
Confessional	Area in which Catholic confesses their sins to a priest so as to receive 'absolution'/forgiveness.
Absolution	The forgiveness of sins pronounced by a priest on behalf of God.
Penance	Act to demonstrate that one is sorry for one's sin.
Stoup	Small vessel of water typically attached to the wall beside the entrance to the church. Finger tips are dipped in the water before making the sign of the cross, indicating that the believer is entering holy ground.

REVISED

Test yourself

(a) Outline **two** significant **features** of a Christian church. (4)
(b) Explain church design and its significance for one denomination. (6)
(c) "Most churches are out-of-date."
Discuss this statement considering the arguments for and against.
   In your answer you should include:
   - reference to teachings
   - other (divergent) points of view – either within the religion or from other religions
   - your opinion/point of view using reasoned arguments
   - a balanced conclusion. (10)

2.3.1b Places of Worship: Baptists

REVISED ☐

GENERIC SYLLABUS
The design and purpose of regional, national or international places of public worship, focused on their internal & external appearances & the status of such buildings in the religion.

CHRISTIAN SYLLABUS
The contrasting design and purpose of two Christian denominations' local places of worship, focused on their internal & external appearances. The historical and contemporary importance of their design. The use of such buildings today and their status in the religion.

Baptist church external appearance: its history.

REVISED ☐

> **Key point**
>
> The Baptist Church was a break-away movement from the Roman Catholic Church, adopting Martin Luther's *"sola scriptura"* (only scripture is necessary for salvation) principle. This Church's buildings are therefore simpler and closer to lecture halls.

- Baptist churches are 'evangelical' due to their focus on the authority of the Bible, personal conversion and salvation by Christ's atonement for our sin on the cross.
- They are a type of Protestant church, accepting Martin Luther's (16th c. AD) rejection of the pope's authority on the basis of his *sola scriptura* principle.
- Baptist churches are therefore built to teach the truths of scripture (the Bible).
- Baptist churches are like lecture-halls. The pulpit (or in more modern churches, the stage) is typically central and elevated. This allows the Baptist Minister to preach God's word.
- To emphasise the importance of personal conversion, Baptist churches also typically include a baptistery (a small swimming pool-like structure). This is used for baptising adults using 'full immersion'. [Baptists reject the Catholic practice of infant baptism and of pouring water over someone's forehead. They claim "real" baptism involves adults personally committing to Christ and fully washing themselves of the sin of their old life.
- To ensure that the focus is on understanding God's word and living according to this, Baptist churches avoid anything that is seen to distract from this , such as art works. There are therefore typically no statues, paintings or elaborate features in the church.

- The Baptist Churches were also significantly influenced by the Reformed Churches (e.g., the Calvinists in Switzerland and Puritans of 16th and 17th century England) who destroyed much of the artistry of the mediaeval churches. They claimed that church artworks were guilty of making 'graven images' of the sacred, condemned in the 10 commandments (Exodus 20).
- In more recent years, Baptists have created 'evangelical' mega-churches, which are complexes that offer a variety of educational and social activities.
- The first 'evangelical' megachurch was the Metropolitan Tabernacle, created in 1861. The Baptist Minister Charles Spurgeon preached to a 6000-seat auditorium.
- Mega-churches have become particularly important in the USA. For example, Elevation Church is a Baptist Evangelical multi-site megachurch in North Carolina. Its weekly church attendance was 27,408 people in 2021 and it has 20 locations, led by Steven Furtick.
- Such mega-churches cater to a wide range of interests, allowing diverse individuals to find a sense of community and support, inspired by a vision of a better life.
- Nevertheless, more local Baptist churches remain important however.

Baptist church internal appearance & its use.

REVISED

> **Key point**
> Features to be found in most Baptist Churches.

- The pulpit is typically central and elevated in Baptist churches so that all the members of the congregation can hear the sermon and see the Minister.
- Traditional items of a Catholic church such as candles, statues, stations of the cross, tabernacles and the confessional.
- Baptist churches are typically decorated with a large cross, which is claimed to celebrate the resurrection, in place of the traditional Catholic crucifix (which is claimed to focus more on the crucifixion).
- The traditional Catholic stone font, used to pour water over the heads of infants or adults, is typically replaced by a swimming pool-like structure. This allows for "believers' baptism", which is the full immersion of adults who repent of their sins and accept Jesus as saviour. There is typically a lid that can be placed over the baptismal pool, allowing the area to be used for a range of functions when baptisms are not taking place.
- Baptist churches might include an altar, but it is typically a modest table and it is not the focus of the church – the pulpit is. The limited importance of the altar is in line with the Baptist rejection of 'transubstantiation' in the eucharist's transubstantiation. [See above.] Baptists rather see the act of communion to be merely symbolic, recollecting Christ's 'last supper'.
- Baptist churches do not focus on creating a sacred space, such as the Catholic chancel, separated from the nave by an altar rail or rood screen. There is rather an open-plan structure, in line with the Baptist church's commitment to the 'priesthood of all believers'.

IGCSE 2 Religious Studies

- Baptist Mega-churches involve a range of sites for socialising, entertainments for children, refreshments, etc. They attempt to bring the Gospel into people's everyday lives by integrating their everyday activities into the church complex.
- Such churches typically reject hymns accompanied by an organ for more contemporary 'worship songs' led by a worship band.
- Unlike Catholic churches therefore, there is not the same emphasis on experiencing the eternal through rituals. The aim of Baptist churches is to bring our everyday lives under God's rule as presented in the Bible: this is the evangelical 'mission' of Baptist churches. Catholic practices are typically seen to be out-of-date or unbiblical and so are rejected.

Local place of worship

REVISED

> **Key point**
>
> The syllabus refers to "local places of worship of any two Christian denominations" and so you should be able to name & describe your local Baptist Church, drawing upon the information here to classify its elements.

- Research your local Baptist place of worship, analysing its features in terms of the traditional features such churches discussed above.
- For example, Cambray Baptist Church is a local Baptist Church in Cheltenham, which exemplifies many of the features of a Baptist Church – a central and elevated pulpit for preaching God's word and balconies to allow as many people as possible to hear and see the Minister's sermon.
- Communion is celebrated on a simple table, which can be moved when convenient.
- There are no statues or pictures. The windows do not include stained glass. There is no confessional, stations of the cross or chancel/sanctuary.
- There are no fixed pews so the church can be used for a range of different purposes – e.g., hosting meals for the congregation.

Baptist Church & 1ˢᵗ evangelical Megachurch

> **Key point**
>
> Baptist characteristics of a church organised around the pulpit and a baptistery for full immersion baptism. Below this is London's Metropolitan Tabernacle, the first evangelical megachurch.

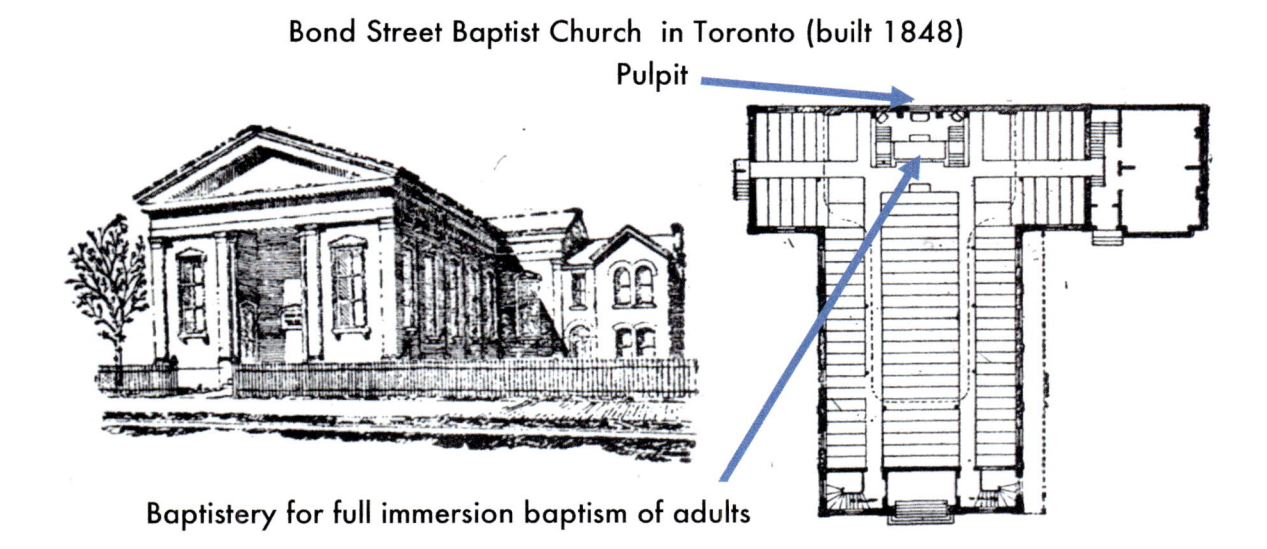

Bond Street Baptist Church in Toronto (built 1848)

Pulpit

Baptistery for full immersion baptism of adults

London Metropolitan Tabernacle (1861) – 1ˢᵗ evangelical mega-church

Pulpit

IGCSE 2 Religious Studies   87

Recall the definitions ... quiz yourself both ways

Key word	Definition
Martin Luther	In 1517, he pinned his '95 theses' to the church door of Wittenberg, Germany, resulting the Reformation. The Baptist Church is one of the many "Protestant" churches created in the Reformation.
Protestant	Churches that separated from the Catholic church following criticisms of church corruption.
Evangelical	Churches focused on the authority of the Bible, personal conversion and salvation by Christ's atonement for our sin on the cross
Baptist	A Protestant and Reformed denomination of Christianity that is evangelical.
Denomination	A type of Christian
Baptistery	A small swimming pool-like structure for full-immersion baptism of adults
Full-immersion	The person being baptised is fully immersed in water rather than having water poured on their forehead.
Believers' baptism	Baptist practice of only baptising adults who have made a personal confession of belief in Christ, employing full immersion.
Priesthood of all believers	Baptist rejection of the distinctions between priests and the laity (congregation) seeing each person to have a personal calling from God.
Laity	Catholic name for those who have not been ordained into the priesthood.
Ministers	Baptist leaders do not claim to share in 'apostolic succession', but to be Ministers, ministering to the needs of their congregation.
Puritans	16th and 17th century English Protestants who destroyed much of the artistry of the mediaeval churches and who influenced the Baptist church.
Metropolitan Tabernacle	First mega-church under Baptist Minister Charles Spurgeon, built in 1861, which included a 6000-seat auditorium.
Elevation Church	A Baptist Evangelical multi-site megachurch in North Carolina, USA, which has a weekly church attendance of 27,408 people in 2021.
Worship Music	Contemporary style music for worship in many Baptist churches, replacing the more traditional use of hymns characteristic of Catholic worship.

TESTED

Test yourself

(a) Outline **two** differences between the external appearances of churches of two different religious communities. (4)

(b) Explain the internal appearances of **two** Christian denominations' local places of worship (6)

(c) "Churches should be used to house the homeless." Discuss.
Discuss this statement considering the arguments for and against.
   In your answer you should include:
   - reference to teachings
   - other (divergent) points of view – either within the religion or from other religions
   - your opinion/point of view using reasoned arguments
   - a balanced conclusion. (10)

231b Places of Worship: Catholicism

88 IGCSE 2 Religious Studies

Topic 2.3.2a Forms of Worship: Catholicism

REVISED

GENERIC SYLLABUS
Forms of public worship and their significance for believers. Forms of regular services and of private devotion and worship; the significance of these for believers.

CHRISTIAN SYLLABUS
Public worship in two denominations of Christianity, focused on the celebration of communion, eucharist, the mass or the Lord's Supper. Rites of passage, and in particular, baptism, marriage & funerals. Private devotional activities & prayer including discussion of their importance. The festivals of Christmas & Easter (already discussed in 2.2.1 above.)

Catholic Mass

REVISED

> **Key point**
>
> The liturgy of the Catholic Mass (communion service) is one of the 7 sacraments.

- The Catholics Mass is the celebration of what other denominations call communion, eucharist or the Lord's Supper: it is the sharing in the body and blood of Christ.
- It is a liturgical form of worship (i.e., with authorised words) that was traditionally performed in Latin. The term 'mass' is taken from the last words of the liturgy: "Ite, missa est" ("Go, it is the sending out]".
- Following the Second Vatican Council (1962–65), the Catholic church typically celebrated communion in the 'vernacular' (local language), but the term 'mass' is still typically used to refer to the celebration.
- Communion is one of the seven sacraments. St Augustine defines a sacrament as the "the visible form of an invisible grace".
- An acronym to remember the 7 sacraments is MR Big COCCe – someone who likes their Coke big. These are Marriage, last Rites, Baptism, Confirmation, Ordination, Communion and Confession.
- Communion is one of the central sacraments since the sacrament of confession (confessing one's sins to a priest) is typically undertaken so as to be spiritually pure for communion. The sacrament of Confirmation is about affirming one's faith in Christ, allowing the Catholic to receive communion. The sacrament of ordination concerns authorising priests and Bishops to preside at communion services and so share the life of God with the congregation.
- Catholics should attend Communion/Mass on holy days of obligation (Sundays and festivals such as Christmas).

- The liturgy of the Mass/Communion involves the following features, divided into three main sections:
  1. PREPARATION: a time of spiritual preparation, including prayers of penitence (saying sorry) and the Gloria in Excelsis (glorifying God). It also includes a 'Collect' (a shared prayer specific to that time in the church calendar or 'lectionary').
  2. LITURGY OF THE WORD: Includes the reading of three main sections of the Bible and the singing of a psalm. It also includes the Nicene Creed and the priest's sermon.
     - Old Testament reading
     - Psalm (sometimes sung by the choir)
     - New Testament letter (epistle)/Acts of the Apostles/Book of Revelation
     - Gospel reading (traditionally read by the priest)
     - Nicene Creed (statement of belief in the Trinity and in the incarnation and virgin birth, which is recited by the congregation)
     - Sermon (traditionally delivered by the priest, relating the Bible reading to the contemporary situation)
  3. LITURGY OF THE SACRAMENT: Includes Old Testament reading or 'lesson' read by member of the congregation
     - Peace (the congregation share the peace by traditionally shaking hands as a sign that there can be no hostility when sharing in the life of God).
     - Prayer of humble access – asking for the humility to meet God in Christ.
     - Prayer of Consecration: the consecration of the elements (bread and wine) in which Jesus' words of 'institution' of the Last Supper are said by the priest: 'Take eat this is my body, which is given for you.' 'Drink this all of you, for this is my blood of the new covenant which is shed for you and for many for the forgiveness of sins.' For Catholics, this is when 'transubstantiation' occurs – when the bread and wine take on the essential natures of the body and blood of Christ.
     - Agnus Dei – 'Lamb of God' prayer, remembering Jesus' sacrifice for our sins in the act of atonement, reconciling us with God.
     - Lord's prayer – Jesus' prayer which is recorded in both Matthew's and Luke's Gospels.
     - Distribution: the body and blood of Christ are shared with all people or sometimes only the body.
     - Prayer of thanksgiving and blessing

Private Prayer

REVISED

> **Key point**
>
> Historical forms of private prayer still practised in the Catholic Church.

- PRAYER: involves bringing one's will into line with God's will – making God's purposes one's own purposes.
- BREVIARY: Catholic priests and monks structure their private prayer in terms of a 'breviary' – a book of prayers including psalms and Bible readings. These prayers were to be recited

- **CHRISTIAN CONTEMPLATION:** a form of prayer that is focused on better understanding the reality of God. A famous example of contemplation from the Eastern Orthodox tradition, which is also used by some Catholics, is the "Jesus prayer". This involves repeatedly praying in harmony with one's breath: 'Lord Jesus Christ, have mercy upon me a sinner.' Through this practice, the believer is claimed to come to a deeper understanding of what it means to wholly depend upon God.
- **CHRISTIAN MEDITATION:** a form of prayer developed by the 16^c AD Catholic priest St Ignatius of Loyola, who was the founder of the Jesuits. Christian meditation is different from what is typically meant by 'meditation' – e.g., developing mindfulness. The focus is not on one's own mind, but on a better understanding of the Biblical events. For example, in his "Spiritual Exercises", Loyola tries to imaginatively identify with different characters' experiences – e.g., the crucifixion experienced from the standpoint of Jesus, Pontius Pilate and Peter.
- **VOTIVE CANDLES:** in churches, there are typically votive candles for the congregation to light for private prayer. The candle's light symbolises the hope that the prayer expresses.
- **ROSARY:** The rosary is a set of beads with a cross attached to it and is used for private prayer, meditating (reflecting) upon the life of Christ so to become more Christ-like. The rosary is part of a liturgical form of prayer, since each element in the rosary is associated with a specific action. For example, when holding the cross, the person praying recites the Apostles' Creed (a key statement of Christian belief). The smaller beads involve reciting Hail Marys – prayers to Mary Mother of Jesus, who is seen to be the 'co-redemptrix' since she shares in God's saving power revealed in Christ. At the larger beads, the Lord's prayer is recited. The rosary also includes beads for meditating upon key events in the life of Christ. There are five key events for each of the following mysteries:
  1. Joyful Mysteries of the Rosary (incarnation)
  2. Sorrowful Mysteries of the Rosary (crucifixion)
  3. Glorious Mysteries of the Rosary (resurrection)
  4. Optional extra set of meditations – the Luminous Mysteries (Jesus' teachings) [added in 2002 by Pope John Paul II]

Praying each mystery involves competing one circuit of the rosary.

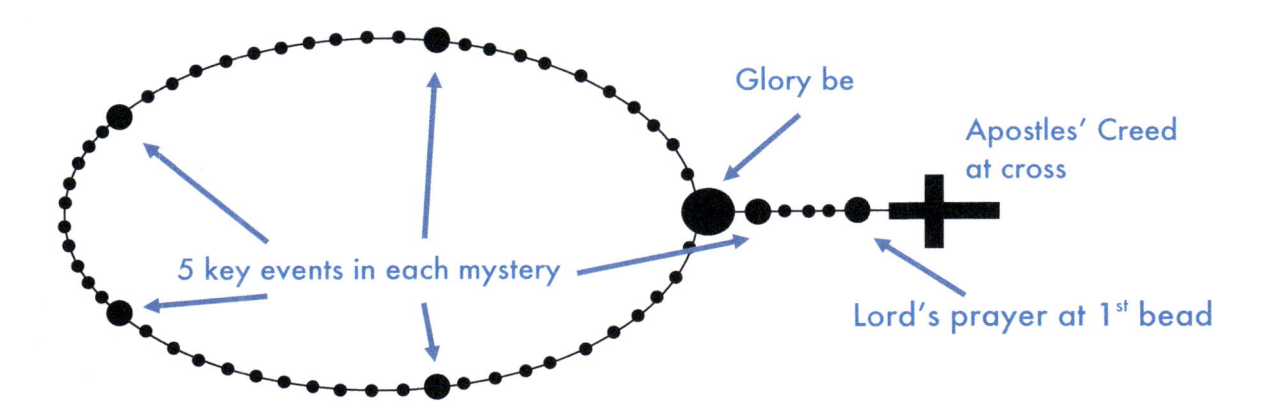

Hail Mary for each smaller bead; there are 10 [a decade] between each mystery

- **SYMBOLISM**: the Catholic Church gives great significance to art for prayer. Different symbols meditate upon different aspects of our relationship to God and they help Catholics to focus their prayers.

SYMBOL	SIGNIFICANCE
Water in baptism	Transformation of character through being washed clean of sin
Dove	Holy Spirit and peace
Crucifix	Self-sacrifice for loved ones, making possible atonement (reconciliation and so peace)
Lamb	The innocent sacrifice
Good Shepherd	Leader who cares for those whom he/she leads
Light/candle	The understanding of God revealed in Christ
White/gold	Colour of vestments (priestly clothing) and altar frontals (coverings of altar) at Christmas and Easter symbolises purity and glory
Christmas presents	Presents symbolise the gift of God's revelation of Himself in his incarnation Jesus.
Easter egg	New life of resurrection
Ash (on Ash Wednesday)	Symbolises that our lives are not eternal and depend upon God
Bread/body & wine/blood	In communion, sharing in the body/blood of Christ symbolises sharing in the life of God by belonging to Christ.
Virgin Mary	Idealised mother, who is claimed to care for her child out of pure love, even giving birth to her child according to God's grace rather than sexual desire.

- **SAINTS**: the Catholic Church encourages intercessory prayer (prayers requesting divine help) through saints. According to the Catholic Catechism (authorised teachings), saints intercede for those who pray to them [i..e, ask God's blessing on those who pray to them] and by their "fraternal [brotherly] concern is our weakness greatly helped". For example, Catholics might pray through Saint Francis of Assisi that they might also be an 'channel of God's peace' as Francis was himself.

Rite of passage 1: Baptism

REVISED

> **Key point**
>
> Catholics typically practise "infant baptism" by pouring water over a child's head from the font so as to wash away sins and so share in the Church of God.

- Rites of passage mark significant events in life – e.g., infant baptism typically marks the birth of a child in Catholicism. Adult baptism involves similar promises to the sacrament of Confirmation for those who have already been baptised: the adult promises to follow the Christian life and 'turn away from sin'.
- Baptism is one of the 7 sacraments of the Catholic

- Baptism is typically performed by an ordained Catholic priest (ordination is another sacrament, the ritual of passing on God's authority to leaders in the church: bishops, priests and deacons).
- The rite of baptism is liturgical – it follows set rituals that have been authorised by Conferences of Bishops for that area. For example, the liturgy of baptism in England needs to be authorised by the Catholic Bishops' Conference of England and Wales.

- **INFANT BAPTISMAL SERVICE** includes:
  1. RECEPTION OF THE CHILD: the priest welcomes the family and godparents at the door of the church asking for the child's name. By baptising the child by name, the church recognises the uniqueness of each person. Traditionally, the name should be that of a saint. One of the godparents should be a practising Catholic.
  2. LITURGY OF THE CATECHUMENATE: Catechumens are people under instruction prior to baptism. In this part of the service, there is a Bible reading and perhaps a sermon by the priest on the significance of the Bible reading and the ritual of baptism. Following this, the priest anoints the child with the oil of catechumens, praying that God blesses the child.
  3. LITURGY OF BAPTISM: in this part of the service, the child is taken to the font, which is traditionally a stone vessel for holding water. Vows are made by the parents on behalf of the child to fight against the devil and to be faithful to God. The water is then blessed by the priest and poured over the child's head three times with the words 'I baptise you in the name of the Father and of the Son and of the Holy Spirit'. The baby is then anointed with the oil of chrism, which is olive oil scented with perfume and blessed by a Bishop. The infant is clothed in white to symbolise their intention to now live a pure life, not corrupted by sin. The infant is given a baptismal candle with the words 'Receive the light of Christ.' This is lit from the Paschal candle (large, decorative Easter candle that stands by the altar).
  4. LITURGY OF BAPTISM: in this part of the service, the child is taken to the font, which is traditionally a stone vessel for holding water. Vows are made by the parents on behalf of the child to fight against the devil and to be faithful to God. The water is then blessed by the priest and poured over the child's head three times with the words 'I baptise you in the name of the Father and of the Son and of the Holy Spirit'. The baby is then anointed with the oil of chrism, which is olive oil scented with perfume and blessed by a Bishop. The infant is clothed in white to symbolise their intention to now live a pure life, not corrupted by sin. The infant is given a baptismal candle with the words 'Receive the light of Christ.' This is lit from the Paschal candle (large, decorative Easter candle that stands by the altar).
  5. BLESSINGS: the service ends with the Lord's prayer and three blessings for the mother, father and friends as they instruct the child in the faith. This takes place at the altar to indicate that God is blessing them through the priest.

- BAPTISM WITHIN MASS: The liturgy of baptism can also be included in a mass, with most of the baptism service occurring before the Liturgy of the Eucharist. The gift of a baptismal candle, lit from the Paschal Candle, is the only element of the baptismal service that occurs after the Liturgy of the Eucharist.

Rite of passage 2: Marriage

> **Key point**
>
> In the Catholic sacrament of marriage, a couple promises to share God's eternal love with one another; it is both a spiritual and legal ceremony.

- Marriage is the rite of passage in which traditionally a man and woman come together to start a family. It involves the couple making vows of loyalty to each other, creating the stability that helps children to grow up in a healthy way.
- Although same-sex marriage is legal in the UK, same-sex marriage is not possible in Catholic churches. The Catholic Catechism (official teaching) states that homosexual relations are "acts of grave depravity" and are "intrinsically disordered." Gay rights activists have protested against this position. For example, Alfredo Ormando burnt himself to death outside Saint Peter's Basilica in Rome in 1998 as: "*a form of protest against a Church that demonises homosexuality*". The UK recognises the church's ability to witness to its beliefs however, and so does not see the church to be guilty of illegal discrimination. Marriages, other than Catholic ones, are also available to homosexuals.
- Similar to baptism, marriage is one of the 7 sacraments performed by an ordained priest according to the set liturgy approved by the Catholic Bishops' Conference.
- Marriage is both a spiritual and legal service (unlike baptism, which is only a spiritual service). Legally, it allows people to be treated as a couple – e.g., a husband might inherit his wife's money in the case of her death.
- BANNS OF MARRIAGE: Prior to the wedding, "banns of marriage" are read out publishing the wedding. This allows legal objections to be raised (e.g., in the UK, marrying more than one spouse is guilty of the crime of bigamy).

- **WEDDING LITURGY**
  1. INTRODUCTORY RITES: welcoming the couple and saying a prayer specific to the sacrament of marriage called a "Collect".
  2. LITURGY OF THE WORD: this includes Bible readings and a sermon by the priest on the significance of marriage and the sacramental vows that the couple are taking.
  3. QUESTIONS BEFORE CONSENT: the priest asks the couple whether they are entering the marriage freely, whether they will love and honour each other and whether they will "accept children lovingly from God and to bring them up according to the law of Christ and his Church".
  4. CONSENT: The Catholic Catechism states that consent "is the indispensable element that 'makes the marriage'". In this part of the service, the couple make marriage vows that they will be faithful to each other "*for better, for worse, for richer, for poorer, in sickness and in health, to love and to cherish, until death do you part?*"
  5. EXCHANGE OF RINGS: rings, whose circular shape is symbolic of eternity, displaying motion without change, are exchanged by the couple as a sign of their undying love for each other. The priest wraps his stole (which is similar to a scarf and symbolises priestly authority) around the couple's hands to show God's sacramental seal on their union.

6. **MARRIAGE BLESSING:** The priest blesses the couple in the name of God, asking that they might be strengthened in their marriage vows.
7. **SIGNING OF THE MARRIAGE REGISTERS:** This is the legal part of the service. The marriage document is signed by the couple and witnesses. This legal document is then sent to the General Register Office for storage.

- **NUPTIAL MASS:** The wedding liturgy can also be included in a mass, in which case it is called a Nuptial Mass. The wedding liturgy comes first followed by Liturgy of the Eucharist.

Rite of passage 3: Funeral

> **Key point**
>
> The funeral service is not a sacrament, but it is an important way of marking how each person is unique to God and shares in eternal life through Christ.

- **RITE OF PASSAGE:** A funeral is a rite of passage, marking the end of someone's life. It is not one of the 7 sacraments. Nevertheless, it is a ritual that is typically performed by a priest in Catholicism.
- **VIGIL:** the body is brought into the church the night before the funeral service. There is a short service to mark receiving the body and loved ones can then pray for the deceased.

- **FUNERAL SERVICE:**
  1. **PROCESSION:** The coffin is typically brought in by "pallbearers" (those responsible for carrying the coffin) and placed before the altar.
  2. **INTRODUCTORY RITES:** the priest greets the congregation and opens the service with a prayer.
  3. **LITURGY OF THE WORD:** includes Bible readings, eulogy (personal recollection of the deceased by a friend or family member) and sermon (the priest's thoughts on the Christian understanding of life's significance).
  4. **COMMENDATION:** the soul is commended to God as the priest sprinkles the coffin with holy water and blesses it with incense.
  5. **COMMITTAL:** After the commendation, the body is taken to the graveyard to be buried or to the crematorium to be burnt. The committal typically takes place there, committing the body either to the ground or to the flames.

- **WAKE:** After the funeral service, there is typically a wake in which family and friends socialise together over drinks and snacks. It is a time for people to remember the deceased and strengthen family and friendship bonds in spite of this loss.
- **REQUIEM MASS:** A funeral service can take place within a mass in which case it is called a Requiem Mass. The priests traditionally wear black vestments and the altar has a black altar frontal (covering). The funeral liturgy comes first and the Liturgy of the Eucharist happens after this. The committal finally takes place outside the church at the graveyard or the crematorium.

Festivals of Christmas & Easter

- For details on the worship of Christmas and Easter, see sections above: 2.2.1 Festivals & Celebrations; (a) Christmas (b) Easter.

Recall the definitions ... quiz yourself both ways

Key word	Definition
Liturgical	Authorised forms of worship, which involve set phrases and actions.
Mass	Catholic term for the eucharist, communion or Last Supper, performed in Latin up till the Second Vatican Council.
Eucharist	Greek for thanksgiving & refers to communion (sharing in life of God by sharing in the body and blood of Christ).
"Ite, missa est"	Last Latin phrase of communion service, meaning "Go, it is the sending out." The word mass is taken from the Latin "missa".
Second Vatican Council	Meeting of Bishops from 1962–65, which reformed Catholicism, including agreeing that the Mass can be performed in the vernacular.
Vernacular	The local language (in contrast to the traditional universal language of Latin)
Sacrament	7 sacred rituals of Catholic Church, including baptism and marriage.
St Augustine	Defined a sacrament as "the visible form of an invisible grace".
Preparation	1st part of the Mass, including penitential prayer or saying sorry and Collect (prayer specific to that time in the church calendar).
Liturgy of the Word	2nd part of the Mass, including Bible readings, Sermon and Nicene Creed.
Liturgy of the Sacrament	3rd part of the Mass, including the central act of consecration in which transubstantiation is said to occur.
Transubstantiation	When the priest says Jesus' words of the Last Supper, the bread takes on the essential nature of Christ's body and the wine takes on the essential nature of Christ's blood.
Prayer	Aligning one's will with the will of God.
Breviary	Authorised prayer book of priests and monks, with set (liturgical) prayers
Contemplative prayer	Prayer focused on understanding one's dependency upon God of which the "Jesus prayer" is a famous example.
Jesus prayer	Involves repeatedly saying, "Lord Jesus Christ, have mercy upon me a sinner" in harmony with one's breath.
Christian Meditation	St. Ignatius of Loyola's practice of imaginatively identifying with a range of Biblical characters so as to appreciate the full significance of an event such as the crucifixion.
St Ignatius of Loyola	Founder of the Order of Jesuits in the 16c AD, who developed the practice of Christian Meditation in his "Spiritual Exercises".
Votive candles	Candles that people praying can light in church to help focus their private prayers.

Key word	Definition
Rosary	Necklace to structure private prayer, including meditating upon 1. the Joyful Mysteries of Incarnation 2. the Sorrowful Mysteries of the Crucifixion 3. the Glorious Mysteries of the Resurrection and 4. the Luminous Mysteries of Jesus' teachings
Symbols	Symbols are important in focusing prayer, such as holding a cross to better appreciate Jesus's sacrifice
Marriage banns	Notifications in church that someone is intending to be married, allowing legal challenges to be made.
Marriage	A rite of passage & 1 of the 7 sacraments of the Catholic church, functioning as both a spiritual and legal service.
Alfredo Ormando	Gay man who burnt himself to death in 1998 in protest against the Catholic position on same-sex couples
Wedding liturgy	1. Introductory rites 2. Liturgy of the Word 3. Questions before consent 4. Consent, expressed through marriage vows 5. Exchange of Rings 6. Blessing 7. Signing of the Marriage Registers (legal)
Nuptial Mass	Marriage service performed within mass
Funeral	A rite of passage, which is not 1 of the 7 sacraments.
Vigil	Receiving the body into church the day before the funeral
Funeral service	1. Introductory rites 2. Liturgy of the Word 3. Commendation of the soul to God 4. Committal of the body to the earth or flames
Wake	Social gathering of the family & friends after the funeral
Requiem Mass	Funeral performed within a Mass

REVISED

Test yourself

Done

(a) Outline **two** rites of passage. (4)
(b) Explain one denomination's understanding of communion. (6)
(c) "Baptism is the most important rite of passage."
Discuss this statement considering the arguments for and against.
   In your answer you should include:
   - reference to teachings
   - other (divergent) points of view – either within the religion or from other religions
   - your opinion/point of view using reasoned arguments
   - a balanced conclusion. (10)

2.3.2b Forms of Worship: Baptists

REVISED

GENERIC SYLLABUS
Forms of public worship and their significance for believers. Forms of regular services and of private devotion and worship; the significance of these for believers.

CHRISTIAN SYLLABUS
Public worship in two denominations of Christianity, focused on the celebration of communion, eucharist, the mass or the Lord's Supper. Rites of passage, and in particular, baptism, marriage & funerals. Private devotional activities & prayer including discussion of their importance. The festivals of Christmas & Easter (already discussed in 2.2.1 above.)

Baptist celebration of Last Supper.

REVISED

> **Key point**
>
> Typically a non-liturgical service, which is seen to be an "ordinance", allowing "believers" to symbolically share in the life of God through Christ.

- **LAST SUPPER:** Unlike the Catholics, the Baptists refer to the act of communion as the Last Supper to emphasise its Biblical basis – its referring to the Jesus' last supper before his crucifixion as recorded in the synoptic Gospels Matthew, Mark and Luke.
- **ORDINANCE:** Baptists do not use the word "sacrament" as it is not in the Bible, due to their seeing the Bible alone to be necessary for salvation. Nevertheless, Jesus himself instructs his disciples to 'take eat' and 'drink this in remembrance of me' and so it is an "ordinance".
- **NO REAL PRESENCE:** The Baptists deny that the 'real presence' of Christ is present in the communion service, as Catholics do Baptists deny that there is any act of transubstantiation at the moment of consecration by the priest. [See above] The service is rather symbolic; in this ordinance, the "kingdom of God" is revealing itself in the Christian community's sharing in the life of God through Christ.
- **REGULARITY:** Whereas Catholics celebrate communion many times a week, and at least every Sunday, Baptists often celebrate the Lord's Supper once a month only.
- **WINE:** Whereas Catholics typically use alcoholic wine for the act of communion, Baptists usually use non-alcoholic wine.
- **NO CHALICE:** Whereas Catholics typically "distribute" communion from a silver chalice (shared cup), Baptist typically have communion from individual shot glasses.
- **DISTRIBUTION:** Whereas the Catholic priest distributes communion to the congregation, in Baptist services the congregation distributes it to each other.
- **NON-LITURGICAL:** Whereas the Catholics have elaborate services in vestments following an authorised liturgy, the Baptist service is informal, trying to evoke the experience of friends breaking bread and drinking together.

Rite of passage 1: Baptism

> **Key point**
>
> Termed "believers' baptism", understood as an "ordinance" for adults to be washed clean of sin by "full immersion" so as to share in the life of God through Christ.

- **ORDINANCE:** As noted above regarding the Last Supper, Baptists do not use the word "sacrament". They do not therefore see baptism to be a sacrament; nevertheless, Baptists do see baptism to be an "ordinance" – a practice introduced by John the Baptist and which Jesus commended his followers to do in his "great commission": "Go and make disciples of all people, baptising them in the name of the Father, the Son and the Holy Spirit." (Matthew 28)

- **INFORMAL:** Although there are agreed practices for celebrating baptism in the Baptist Church, there is not the formal liturgy of the Catholic Church. For example, the Baptist service involves no priest anointing candidates with holy oils (oils of the catechumenate and oils of chrism). Instead, the Minister adopts a typically less formal approach.

- **ADULT BAPTISM:** Baptists reject infant baptism in favour of "believers' baptism" – baptism is the washing away of sin so as to accept God's grace, and this can only be done through feeling truly sorry for one's sins. Infants are not able to do this, being too young, and so the Baptists only baptise adults. Baptists do not see the Catholic practice of infant baptism to be valid and so Catholics, converting to the Baptist denomination, need to be rebaptised.

- **DEDICATION SERVICE:** For those parents wanting a service to thank God for their child and to make promises to bring the child up in the faith, Baptists can have a Dedication Service in place of the infant baptism service of Catholicism.

- **TESTIMONY:** Adults are typically encouraged to make a personal testimony in their baptism to show that they truly repent of any sin they have committed and how they are now committed to following in the path of Christ.

- **FULL IMMERSON:** Adults are baptised by going fully under water under the guidance of the Minister. For this purpose, churches often have a small pool ("baptistry") towards the front of the church with a covering to allow people to walk over it. This covering is removed when conducting a baptismal service.

- **WHITE GARMENT:** The Minister and baptismal candidate typically wears a white gown for baptism to mark its role in spiritual purification.

- **RITE OF PASSAGE:** As a rite of passage therefore, baptism in the Baptist church marks someone's coming to spiritual maturity and so their being able to commit to a higher purpose then that of personal satisfaction – a commitment to sharing in the will of God as revealed in Christ.

IGCSE 2 Religious Studies

Rite of passage 2: Marriage

> **Key point**
>
> Not an "ordinance", like the Last Supper and baptism, but a service celebrating a couple's sharing in the life of God through commitments of eternal love.

- **SERVICE:** As noted above regarding the Last Supper, Baptists do not use the word "sacrament" and so do not see marriage to be a sacrament. Jesus also do not command his followers to marry and so marriage is not an "ordinance" (as the Last Supper and Baptism are). Nevertheless, Jesus holds marriage in high regard, emphasising how the bond of marriage should be monogamous (someone should not have multiple spouses at the same time) and life-long (someone should not leave their spouse to marry someone else). The marriage service marks vows of such life-long commitment.

- **INFORMAL:** Baptist services are typically less formal than Catholic ones and do not follow the authorised liturgy of the Catholic Bishops' Conference. Ministers have some freedom in crafting their own services, although the services are meant to be Bible-based, following Martin Luther's "*sola scriptura*" principle (the guidance of scripture alone is necessary for salvation). The Minister typically does not wear the vestments (special clothing) of the Catholic priest and it would be very rare to combine a marriage with a communion service (as is the case with a Catholic Nuptial Mass).

- **BIBLE READINGS:** The Baptist service would not use the language of the Liturgy of the Word, but it would typically involve Bible readings so as to situate the couple's commitment to each other within the broader commitment of God to His people.

- **SERMON:** The Baptist Minister would typically preach on the significance of marriage, and on the challenge to remain true to one's marriage vows.

- **CONSENT:** The marriage service involves freely committing oneself to another person in the power of God's love. Making such commitment in marriage vows are therefore important parts of a Baptist marriage service, similar to a Catholic one.

- **RINGS:** Similar to the Catholic service, marriage typically involves the exchange of rings by the couple. The Minister wears no stole (symbol of priestly authority) however and so cannot wrap this around the hands of the couple.

- **NO BLESSING:** Accepting the 'priesthood of all believers', Baptists do not see priests to have the authority to bless people on God's behalf and so there is typically no formal blessing in a Baptist service.

- **SIGNING OF THE REGISTERS:** Similar to a Catholic service, marriage involves both spiritual and legal promises. The "Signing of the Registers" is also therefore present in a Baptist marriage, so that spouses have the legal rights of marriage (e.g., joint care of any children and inheritance rights in case of one of the spouse's deaths).

Rite of passage 3: Funeral

> **Key point**
>
> Not an "ordinance", but a service by which Baptists give thanks for the life of a person in a typically less liturgical way than Catholic funerals.

- **CHURCH OR CREMATORIUM:** If the deceased is a practising member of the Baptist Church, the service often takes place in the church itself. If the deceased was not practising and is to be cremated (burnt) then the service can take place in the crematorium itself.

- **RITE OF PASSAGE:** A funeral is a rite of passage, marking the end of someone's life. Funerals were commanded by Christ to his disciples in the Bible so they are not seen as "ordinances".

- **MINISTER:** The Baptist Minister (not "priest") typically leads the service.

- **INFORMAL:** The Baptist Church does not have a centralised authority similar to Catholicism's "Magisterium" [authoritative teaching body] under the supervision of the Pope. There is therefore no set liturgy for services and there can be significant regional variations. Nevertheless, services tend to be less "elaborate" than Catholic services and more informal. Robes (vestments) and ancient rituals (e.g., the use of incense) are typically absent.

- **FUNERAL SERVICE:**
  1. PROCESSION: The coffin is typically brought in by "pallbearers" (those responsible for carrying the coffin) and placed at the front of the church (rather than before the altar as with a Catholic service).
  2. WELCOME: The Baptist Minister, typically wearing a suit, rather than the vestments (robes) of a Catholic priest, welcomes the people informally. This welcome does not include the
  3. BIBLE READING: although there is no formal 'liturgy of the word' in Baptist services, there are Bible readings.
  4. EULOGY: Someone who knows the deceased will often reflect upon that person's life, giving thanks for their character and gifts.
  5. SERMON: The Minister will often reflect upon the significance of death in terms of the Christian commitment to "faith, hope and love". (1 Corinthians 13)
  6. COMMENDATION & COMMITTAL: Baptist services typically involve some form of commending the deceased soul to God and of committing the body to the ground (burial) or flames (cremation). There is no set liturgy for this however – only "examples" that Ministers choose to follow.

- **WAKE:** Similar to Catholic services, after the funeral service, there is typically a wake in which family and friends socialise together over drinks and snacks. It is a time for people to remember the deceased and strengthen family and friendship bonds in spite of this loss.

- **NOT CELEBRATED WITH LORD'S SUPPER:** It is very rare for a Baptist funeral service to be included with the Lord's Supper as occurs in the Catholic Requiem Mass. This is because communion does not have the central significance that it has for Catholics.

Festivals of Christmas & Easter

REVISED ☐

- For details on the worship of Christmas and Easter, see sections above: 2.2.1 Festivals & Celebrations; (a) Christmas (b) Easter.

Recall the definitions ... quiz yourself both ways

TESTED ☐

Key word	Definition
Baptist Church	Denomination of Christianity focused on the authority of scripture rather than on traditional figures of authority (e.g., priests).
Minister	Baptist leaders are called Ministers as they do not claim to share in divine authority through "apostolic succession", but simply minister to the need of the congregation to understand God's word (scripture).
Last Supper	Baptist term for communion, focused on its Biblical basis (its being the last supper Jesus had).
Ordinance	The Baptist Church rejects the 7 sacraments as having no Biblical basis, but sees celebrating the Last Supper and Baptism to be Jesus' "ordinances" or requirements for his disciples.
Symbolic	Baptists do not see the Last Supper to involve the "real presence" of Christ as Catholics believe happens with transubstantiation [see above]. The service is rather symbolic, allowing believers to imaginatively share in the life of God through Christ.
Regularity	Baptists typically celebrate the Last Supper once a month whereas Catholics celebrate it at least once a week.
Wine	Baptists often use non-alcoholic wine and individual shot glasses (rather than a shared chalice).
Distribution	Baptists often share communion with each other according to their belief in the "priesthood of all believers".
Non-liturgical	The Baptist Church does not have a central authority to agree liturgy and so individual Ministers celebrate the Last Supper as they see fit.
Rite of passage	A ritual marking a stage in life's journey (e.g., baptism marking spiritual maturity, marriage marking starting a family & a funeral marking death).
Baptism	Washing away sin following the practice of John the Baptist and an "ordinance" of Christ (Matthew 28)
Dedication Service	There is no "infant baptism" in the Baptist Church, but there are "dedication services" to dedicate a child to sharing in God's will through Christ.
Believers' Baptism	The Baptist Church sees baptism to involve a personal sense of guilt and a need for God's grace. Infants cannot properly experience this radical responsibility and so Baptists only baptise adults.
Full Immersion	Baptists fully immerse baptismal candidates (rather than pour water over the head of the candidate as occurs in the Catholic Church).
Baptistry	A small pool for baptising baptismal candidates in Baptist Churches.

Key word	Definition
Garment	White garments often worn by Minister and baptismal candidate in full immersion baptisms.
Marriage	A service (rather than sacrament or ordinance) in which a couple makes spiritual and legal promises to loyally love each other in agreement with Christ's commitment to loving monogamous relations.
Monogamy	Marriage between just two spouses.
Bigamy	Marrying multiple people at the same time is judged to be a crime (e.g., polygamy is seen to be guilty of bigamy in the UK).
Crematorium	An area in which funeral services can be conducted and in which bodies are burnt after the service. Crematoria often have gardens around them so that the ashes can then be "interred" (e.g., placed by a tree) so that family and friends have somewhere to visit when remembering the deceased.
Burial ground	Area in which bodies are "interred" or buried
Interred	Either a body or ashes are placed in the ground, allowing a place for family and friends to visit to remember the deceased.
Pallbearers	People who carry the coffin into and out of the church/crematorium.
Commendation	Commending the soul to God.
Committal	Committing the body to the ground (burial) or the flames (cremation).
Eulogy	Personal account of the deceased, typically by a friend or family member.
Sermon	Spiritual understanding of death in the light of the Christian commitment to "faith, hope and love" (1 Corinthians 13)
Wake	A time for family and friends to gather after the funeral to remember the deceased and comfort each other. This typically occurs in a coffee shop or restaurant.

REVISED

Test yourself

(a) Outline **two** parts of a marriage service. (4)
(b) Explain two different denomination's understanding of baptism. (6)
(c) "The particular form of the celebration of the Eucharist is not important."
Discuss this statement considering the arguments for and against.
   In your answer you should include:
   - reference to teachings
   - other (divergent) points of view – either within the religion or from other religions
   - your opinion/point of view using reasoned arguments
   - a balanced conclusion. (10)

Credits

- Cover picture of "The Arrest of Christ (Kiss of Judas)" by Giotto di Bondone of the Scrovegni Chapel, Padua; in the public domain.
- Pictures of the Church of the Nativity, Bethlehem & of the Church of the Holy Sepulchre, Jerusalem are from: Fletcher, Banister (1946) *A History of Architecture: on the Comparative Method* (17th ed.), New York: Charles Scribner's Sons ISBN: 0750622679, now in the public domain.
- Vatican City Map © Wikimedia Commons User: Vatican City picture courtesy of Thomas Römer/OpenStreetMap data / CC-BY-SA-3.0, made available by ©OpenStreeMap contributors under the Open Database License (ODbL).
- Architectural drawings of Miriam Samuel.
- Fr. Robert Wright of All Saints, Cheltenham for permission to photograph his church.
- Image of Bond Street Baptist Church, Toronto from image displayed by Toronto Public Library, now in public domain: http://www.torontopubliclibrary.ca/detail.jsp?Entt=RDMDC-PICTURES-R-3509&R=DC-PICTURES-R-3509
- Image of The Metropolitan Tabernacle Pulpit 1864 in the public domain.

Printed in Great Britain
by Amazon